LEAPING BEYOND THE VISION

> *"DESTINY is not created by what chair we sit in, what watch we wear, what shoes we wear or what mobile phone we have*
>
> But
>
> *How we make decisions by sitting in the chair, how we use time using the watch, what steps we take towards the goal and how we communicate using any communication medium"*

EFFECT OF TANGIBLE AND INTANGIBLES IN PROJECT MANAGEMENT: CASE STUDIES

Cdr Dr. VIVEKANAND BANKOLLI

Late Hon. **Lt. Mallikarjun. R. Bankolli**
(Indian Army)

— **Unsung Hero** —

Who not only cared for living existences but also its
supporting entity

"The Nature."

About Author –

Cdr Dr. Vivekanand M Bankolli (Retd), PMP

Cdr Dr. Vivekanand M Bankolli was parented by a hardcore army soldier who encouraged him to join defence forces to serve the nation alongside his brother. His family has contributed more than seventy six years plus (and is continuing) to the nation in just two generations. Post his short stint of ten years, Vivekanand moved to corporate to pursue and excel in his passion for project management.

Vivekanand is basically a Mechanical graduate; however, along with his professional career, he continued to sharpen the skills necessary for project management. He holds International Executive Diploma in project management from George Washington University (including training at NASA), Certificate in project management (CIPM), project risk management (CePRM), Complex project management (CeCPM), Qualified project management professional since 2007, General management program (Operations & Finance) from Indian Institute of Management Lucknow, Marine Engineering Professional Course from Indian Navy (First in the Course), Post Graduate Diploma in Marketing Management from Symbiosis Institute of Management Studies, Lean Six Sigma Black belt, also he is Doctorate in project management from Indian Institute of Technology (Bombay)

Vivekanand is an accomplished multifaceted techno-commercial professional known for situational strategic business solutions. He has a total of twenty nine years of experience, which includes ten years in defence and ninteen years in corporate. His corporate experiences arrays in the fields of Projects, Operations, Supply chain, Strategic, Financial and Facilities management. In his corporate tenure, he worked with Larsen & Toubro, Wartsila India, Oil States India Pvt Ltd, Jones Long Lassalle and presently he is CEO of Jolle Group.

Vivekanand became passionate about project management since his first corporate exposure as a project trainee. The 'eureka' feeling from the dynamics of project challenges made him pursue the levels beyond his reach. That is how he designated his book as "Leaping Beyond the Vision," the phenomenon which could have been experienced by many of the readers also.

While in corporate he identified lag between the academia and corporate sector business affairs conversely the adaptation of the academia researched concepts by the corporates, hence he pursued study in the project domain of operation management. This led him to write a book which can help academia as well as corporates to understand the dynamics of corporates for the efficacy of the project system. He has presented real case scenarios there by making it as a unique type of hybrid book which is deviant from traditional form of books for both corporate sector and academia.

This book is being published with philosophy that readers gain from the learnings of success and failure from other experiences and leap forward rather than going through the same experiences.

Thus enabling them to proceed further in their professional career and contributing with higher efficacy quotient towards their organisation, country, and society as a whole.

He has published & presented six research papers at various national and international forums. Under his leadership, Magnum tuff was awarded the best company in north Karnataka within two years of starting its operations. He has been awarded a Leadership Award by MoRe Global Organization in 2023 and again in 2024.

Mr. Subhash Tyagi

Chairman and the Chief Promoter of
Gold Plus Glass Industry Limited.

INDIAN PATRIOT LEADER WITH BUSINESS VISIONARY, who has been implementing 'Atmanirbhar' & 'Make in India' concept since 1985 is none other than Mr. Subhash Tyagi. Rare trait that makes him stands out from others global business leaders, is one who is attached with ground and capability of flying high in the sky beyond reach. He is achieving the feat through scaling up the business by forward integration in the glass industry and still going strong. He has given employment to 3800 plus in his group of organizations, 20000 plus in the associated supply chain formal sector. Multiple factories built by him have not only developed the nearby area but also in developed the respective state and country. In addition, the employment generated due to the other sectors/ industries cannot be ascertained.

Mr. Subhash Tyagi the Chairman and the Chief Promoter of Gold Plus Glass Industry Limited. He started his journey in the glass industry in 1985 as a glass trader and continued to grow till he became the largest glass trader in the country in the early 90's. He Established Gold Plus Glasses India Limited, a glass processing plant in Sonepat, Haryana, in 1996. By 2004 Gold Plus became the largest glass processor in the country in architectural segment. In 2009 Gold Plus started float glass manufacturing in Roorkee and under his guidance has now become the second largest float glass manufacturer in the country. He was the founder director of Federation of Safety Glass. He has previously served as the director of All-India Glass Manufacturers Federation and has also chaired the Architectural Glass Panel at the All-India Glass Manufacturers' Federation.

Mr. Tyagi is a firm believer of conducting business with highest Corporate Governance standards. He has been passionate about environmental sustainability and social welfare and has inculcated and made sustainability and CSR integral parts of Gold Plus Group. His guidance and contribution have enabled Gold Plus Group to make significant difference and progress on the right path.

The project of glass manufacturing plant at Kanagla (Belgaum, Karnataka) of 1900 tons/day capacity (1600 float & 300 solar) has achieved the schedule success criteria in world record's time. The schedule was improved by around fourteen months for single float line and aim is to improve the schedule of three lines significantly. This project is supposed to be the best example and the essence of this book on project management. I would like to present Mr. Tyagi as an inspirational leader, not only as a project management professional but also in other domains of management, for leading business to levels which could be termed as "Leaping Beyond the Vision." His exceptional success in the field of business inspired me to write this book for the benefit industry practitioners as well as management students.

Preface

In a world where technology is advancing at an unprecedented pace, it is becoming prudent for us to explore the limits of human potential. Our ability to see beyond the realm of what is immediately apparent to us is not only a remarkable trait but a necessary one for our progression in the corporate business world for society.

In our book, Leaping Beyond Vision – case studies, we aim to take readers on a journey of discovery, challenging conventional notions of what is possible and delving into the depths of our imagination. Exploring the dynamics of project management and the power of the mind, team and integration. We intend to inspire readers to tap into their own abilities and test beyond full potential. From the world of virtual reality to the exploration of outer space, we will delve into some of the most exciting advancements in science and technology and highlight how our ability to think beyond the limitations of reality is driving progress in management disciple.

Leaping Beyond Vision is not just a book about technology and innovation. It is a call to action, urging readers to embrace their own creativity and tenacity in the pursuit of their dreams which is found within the individuals and as group, by cultivating the ability to see beyond the goals set.

The intention of the book is to make the individual and team understand their capacity and capability beyond their perceived limits. If we converge our self-efforts individually along with the team, it is possible to achieve results beyond set targets/ goals which results in, what can be termed as leaping beyond our vision. The best way to understand the phenomenon is through case studies. Therefore, the case studies presented in this book helps in understanding the pragmatic and holistic approach which shall enable individual and the team to achieve results beyond set expectations.

We can correlate to our own experiences, when we had finished our education and stepped into the professional world (corporate world), most of us were unable to realise the correlation between the academic orientation towards the professional requirements. Though the basic concepts remained the same, the implementation approach changed, mainly due to the context in which industries operate. This causes a lag between the academics and the requirement of industries. This is where the seed of bridging the gap between the academia and professional/ corporate occurred to us.

The germination of seed commenced while we as a team started achieving beyond the set goals/ targets. However, not understood the phenomenon, until stepped into the professional world and realised the strength of the human mind. Implementation of structured and organized concepts in live projects indicated that if energies are converged, then organisations probability of achieving success of the set goal (subset of vision) non-only increases but also goes beyond the objectives (project goals). While in the professional/ corporate world there were many instances wherein, as a team we achieved beyond set objectives and anticipated outcome, the contributory factors for such outcome were intangible in nature which played the role of catalyst for the tangible outputs. The experience was something beyond the "eureka" moment, since eureka effect is solution for anticipated result of a problem. As a team we realised several such instances where in, not only our organisation but also the channel partners were able to achieve beyond their set vision. Hence it was intended to explore the dynamics for such instances and the reason for the unanticipated results. Series of such events, where unexpected results were achieved was inclusive of several failures gave the thought of identifying the causes or factors influencing outcomes. Therefore, in this book polar case studies have been considered for the readers to understand the successful and failure Project.

Project management is one of the most sought domain expertise since it being the building block for all programmes and portfolios. The revenues are generated not only from the projects but also from the operations from the completed project which supplement to the organisational goal and vision. Therefore, the study was undertaken to increase the efficacy of the project system, wherein findings from the analysis indicate that interplay of right set of success factors shall provide success beyond our vision.

This e-book/ book compiles live case studies providing the insights and dynamics of the project management. This will be helpful to all the project practitioners to understand the in-depth dynamics of projects to corelate with their own project for enhancement of the project performance. In addition, this can be helpful for the technical and management academic students in understanding the real case scenarios, enabling them to practice in their own projects being undertaken for the industries.

The questionnaire of the case studies evolved post exploratory study of factors influencing project success and pilot case study for case study itself. Questionnaire, results, analysis, conclusion, etc... of the case studies are compiled as complete book – 'Leaping Beyond the Vision - Effect of Tangible and Intangible Factors in project management.'

Reading this book shall help the organisations and the business leaders to expand their vision horizon for transforming their business as intended by germinating the idea with constant change in the growth.

Abstract

SUCCESSFUL PROJECT COMPLETIONS ENABLES organisations to achieve the set success criteria, however this success has limited benefits and prevents organisations from realising higher objectives. Though, project management came into existence around 5000 years back, nonetheless organisation began to understand its significance and started gaining the benefits only since past sixty five years. Project management started evolving since 1950 at a rapid pace to the changing demands of the business requirements, yet most of the projects do not achieve the desired success of cost, time, and scope. Further, few projects, despite meeting these success criteria, stakeholders are not satisfied with the results. Therefore, the need to enhance the project performance has become essential for practitioners and in the interest of academic domain at various levels.

Most of the studies undertaken are from the construction industry, with less focus on the success or failure factors in marine projects (shipbuilding and oil and gas sector). Further, in Indian marine industry there are no formal studies undertaken with regards to the factors influencing the project success or failure. Therefore, a study was undertaken to identify the success criteria and success factors responsible for the project success or failure and verify the adequacy of the present success criteria; cost, time, scope, and quality (Iron triangle). To recognise the insufficiencies in present practice, philosophy of exploratory, inductive phenomenological based qualitative methodology was conducted by means of case studies.

The study was undertaken in two stages, in the first stage, interview with the project participants to identify the success criteria and success factors that affect the project success. In the second stage, empirical based five case studies were undertaken to validate the identified factors and check for additional factors and success criteria if any? These cases were evaluated for the "iron triangle" as success criteria and as per the perception of project participants. This book is independent of the complete study undertaken, thereby enabling readers to understand the cases with independent evaluation and arrive at an optimal approach. Hence this book is self-regulating and subset to the complete study undertaken as mentioned earlier. The case studies will enable young project professionals to understand the dynamics of the project. In addition, these cases shall be helpful not only for professional & management students but also other undergraduate and post graduate students who would like to understand the essence of organisational dynamics and evaluate the cases for the possible solutions.

Readers will understand the insufficiencies and the essentials present project management practices and can be correlated to interplay of the various factors which can be distinctly categorized. Therefore, one will be able to analyse the cases independently and combinedly for factors governing the success factor and criteria. The interrelationship of these factors plays a vital role in project success or failure, as these factors are present and veiled in the project management processes thereby influencing the project's performance.

After reading the cases the reader should be able to make out the relationship between the success criteria and factors and how they are mutually exclusive and inclusive based on the criteria and factors. Furthermore, they will be able to define their own success criteria and factors for their respective organisations or as a student will be able to provide the analysis and suggestions in the study undertaken.

The final study (book – Leaping Beyond the Vision) concludes mainly with the success criteria, success factors and other attributes influencing the project success for Indian marine industry which can be evaluated and appropriately considered for other industries. Inclusion of these factors into present practices will enhance project performance, since identified factors were derived from the project practitioners thereby contributing to present practices. The study demonstrates that end user project objectives are vital and these need to be integrated with other success criteria for a project to be successful with respect to tangible as well as intangible factors.

Keywords: Success criteria, success factors, project performance, marine projects, tangible and intangible factors

Index

List of Tables

List of Figures

Abbreviations

API - American Petroleum Institute

BOE - Barrel of Oil equivalent

CCA - Cross Case Analysis

COO - Chief Operating Officer

CSL - Cochin Shipyard Limited

EPCI - Engineering, Procurement, Construction and Installation

EPCM - Engineering, Procurement, Construction and management

EPM - Engineering, Procurement and management

EU - European Union

FAT - Factory Acceptance trials

GTOSI - G and T Oil States Industries Pvt. Ltd

IMO - International Maritime Organisation

JV - Joint Venture

JVP - Joint Venture Partner

IPMA - International project management association

L1 - Lowest One

LCA - Life-Cycle Analysis

LCC - Life-Cycle Costing

LD - Liquidated Damages

MARPOL - Marine Pollution

MECO - Material, Energy, Chemical and Other

MPE - Markov Perfect Equilibrium

MSP - Microsoft project

OEM - Original Equipment Manufacturer

ONGC - Oil and Natural Gas Corporation Ltd.

OS - Organisation Structure

OSSS - Oil States Skagit SMATCO

PBOs - Project Based Organisations

PCP - Procurement complex performance

PM - Project management

PMI - Project management institute

PMBOK - Project Management Book of knowledge

PP - Project Participants

PPf - Project Performance

RFP - Request for Proposal

TCE - Transaction Cost Economics

OEM - Original Equipment Manufacturer

SAT - Site Acceptance Trials

SAT[1] - Sea Acceptance Trials

SCI - Shipping Corporation of India

SHA - Stakeholder Analysis

STP - Sewage Treatment Plant

WCA - Within Case Analysis

Glossary

Project - Project is a temporary endeavour undertaken to create a unique product, service, or result. The temporary nature indicates a definite beginning and end.

Project management - Is the application of Knowledge, skills, tools, and techniques to project activities to meet the project requirements.

Project channel members - Project is undertaken to produce a unique product for the end customer/user. The organisations / Companies involved in the procurement channel for accomplishment of end-user product.

Project performance - Degree to which the actual project success criteria has been achieved against the planned set criteria. Mapping the dimensions of project success.

Success criteria - Criteria/Specific parameters set against which the performance is measured.

Success factors (SF) - Factors or activities which affect the project success and are required for ensuring the project success.

Critical success factor (CSF) - Factors or activities which are vital and essential to ensure the project success.

Deliverable – Any unique and verifiable product, result, or capacity to perform a service that must be produced to complete a process, phase, or project. However, often used more narrowly in reference to an external deliverable, which has approval from project sponsor or customer.

Environmental Factor - Any or all internal and external factor that surrounds or influences the project. These factors are from any or all of the enterprises involved in the project. These factors may enhance or constrain project management options and can have positive or negative influence on the project outcome.

Change Control Board (CCB) - A formally constituted group of stakeholders responsible for reviewing, evaluating, approving, delaying, or rejecting changes to a project.

Retrofit projects - These are maintenance projects, where the major systems are replaced with new systems for improving the product life cycle and the performance of the product. The replacements are normally undertaken at the site, or onboard ship, vessel, or platform.

Introduction

Marine Industry and Projects

It is well known that about 71 percent of the Earth's surface is water-covered, and the oceans hold about 96.5 percent of all Earth's water. Therefore, the ocean plays significant role in global economics of business requirements that necessitates programmes, research & developments in several domains of economics, marine environment, ecology etc.

The global marine industry contributes to approximately 18 - 21% of global GDP (based on various surveys) and is increasing year on year. The industry encompasses a broad range of sectors, each playing a crucial role in international trade, transportation, defence, resource exploration, environment, food, marine life, ecological, etc... Here is a brief overview:

Shipping and Maritime Transportation:

The shipping industry is a vital component of the global economy, responsible for the transportation of goods and commodities across the world's oceans. Key players include container shipping companies, bulk carriers, oil tankers, and specialised vessels for various industries.

- **Shipbuilding and Repair:** Shipbuilding involves the construction of ships, ranging from small vessels to large container ships and oil tankers. Major shipbuilding nations include China, South Korea, and Japan, with several other countries also contributing significantly.

- **Port Operations and Infrastructure:** Ports serve as crucial nodes in the global supply chain, facilitating the loading and unloading of cargo between ships and land-based transportation. Investments in port infrastructure, automation, and efficiency are ongoing trends in the industry.

- **Oil and Gas Exploration:** The marine industry plays a vital role in the exploration, extraction, and transportation of oil and gas resources. Offshore drilling platforms, floating production storage and offloading (FPSO) units, and support vessels are essential components of this sector.

- **Maritime Technology and Innovation:** Advances in technology, including autonomous vessels, digitalisation, and the use of big data, are transforming the maritime industry. Innovations in navigation, communication, and safety systems contribute to operational efficiency and sustainability.

- **Fisheries and Aquaculture**: The global marine industry includes the fishing sector, with both industrial and small-scale fisheries contributing to the production of seafood. Aquaculture, or the farming of fish and other aquatic organisms, is another growing segment of the industry.

- **Environmental Sustainability**: The marine industry faces increasing scrutiny regarding its environmental impact. Efforts to reduce emissions, adopt cleaner technologies, and address issues such as ballast water management are ongoing.

- **Cruise and Tourism:** The cruise industry caters to millions of passengers each year, offering leisure and travel experiences. The sector has faced challenges, including those related to safety, environmental concerns, and the impact of global events such as the COVID-19 pandemic.

- **Maritime Security**: Maritime security is a critical aspect of the industry, encompassing measures to combat piracy, ensure vessel safety, and protect against other maritime threats.

- **International Regulations and Governance**: The industry is subject to various international regulations and conventions aimed at ensuring safety, environmental protection, and the fair treatment of seafarers. It's important to note that the global marine industry is dynamic, and developments may have occurred since my last update. For the latest information, it is recommended to refer to recent industry reports, news sources, and official

The marine projects are undertaken for the various subdomains of the subsectors as stated earlier. However, in our context we shall consider the Engineering Maine projects which further are classified under Commercial & Defence (Navy) for construction projects of defence and oil & gas sector.

Marine shipbuilding projects are complex in nature due to multiple stake holders involved, safety requirements, quality requirements, international & domestic statutory requirements, latest technology, lifesaving equipments & apparatus, human resources involved. In addition, if the projects are of defence or oil & gas, the complexity increases. Therefore, in this study, mix of complex projects from both defence and oil & gas have been considered for understanding the dynamics from the marine industry.

Case Studies

Case study is known as one of the best research methods of study in various fields, mainly in business scenarios to get empirical results. It helps professionals to understand the organisational business dynamics encompassing, inter, intra and environment. The study involves an in-depth examination of a single subject or a small group of subjects to gain a deeper understanding of a specific phenomenon or problem.

Case studies typically involve gathering data from multiple sources, such as interviews, observations, documents, archival records, etc... This data is then analysed and interpreted to identify patterns, themes, and insights. The purpose of a case study can vary depending on the field of study and research objectives. This method also provides platforms to explore a theoretical framework, provide practical insights and solutions for real-world problems, or highlight unique or exceptional cases. Case studies offer several advantages as a research method. It provides an opportunity to study complex and contextual phenomena in their natural settings and capture rich and detailed data. They can also reveal new and unexpected findings and generate hypotheses for further research.

However, case studies do have limitations such as, findings may not be generalised to the broader population, potential for bias in data collection, interpretation and it being time-consuming and resource intensive. Despite this limitation the study provides best results which are empirical in nature and have ground zero information, nevertheless, the limitations can be overcome by multibrid studies which has been undertaken in this study.

The research methodology adopted to conduct this study was both qualitative and quantitative in nature. The first phase comprised semi-structured interviews with marine project practitioners to identify the tangible and intangible factors that influence the project performance. The second phase is comprised of multiple case studies.

This book comprises the cases undertaken in the second phase of the whole study undertaken for the objective set. To refute the initial variances of the questionnaire set and to ensure the same validates for appropriate data collection, the case studies were undertaken in two stages. In the first stage, an exploratory study (Reiter, 2013) using semi-structured interviews was carried out involving fifteen project practitioners as a pilot study from thirteen different organisations. In the final Stage II, the survey was extended to ninty two project practitioners for the main study. The respondents are project practitioners from different organisations in the marine industry and are from both public and private limited companies. Selection of the organisations was done to represent sampling from deviant organisations within the industry, sampling of maximum variation and for a specific criterion (industry).

In Stage II, five cases from the marine industry fulfilling theoretical and literal replication logic were selected with polar type cases. The selected cases include two successful projects, two unsuccessful projects and one project perceived as successful (based on customer satisfaction). The cases selected represent shipbuilding and oil & gas sectors of the marine industry with different types of deliverables expected of newly built and the retrofit type of projects. This was to ensure that the cases represent a balanced mix of projects and a proportionate representation. 25 to 40 project participants from the respective project teams were considered for the discussions and gather the case data. Secondary sources of data were also used for case development.

The case studies are likely to benefit both academic and corporate practitioners, not only to the Indian marine industry but also to other industries. The analysis by the individual reader will help them in finding optimal solutions for their own projects or organisation. Analyzing the case studies will help them in evaluating projects for the vital success factors thereby increasing the probability of the project success. As a contribution to theory/ academicians, understanding the case studies and their influence towards project success through project management by correlating these cases to their (readers) own cases. The reason being, very few studies in specific sectors (in this case marine industry) have been undertaken in the past. Additionally, this study offers novel insights into the management of projects in the Indian context which can be integrated with the current PM practices and same can also be extended and benchmarked with other industries.

Based on the case studies, project professionals & students should be able to answer questions related to the project success criteria, factors, and their role in project performance. Though the study is based on marine industry, same can be extended to the other industries and generalisation can be checked for other industries, since the success criteria usually remains same and common success factors present the organisations system. However, the importance of the success factors in terms of applicability may change as per the industries.

Methodology

METHODOLOGY ADAPTED DEFINES THE effectiveness, accuracy, and reliability of the results, therefore the study undertaken needs to be carried out in structured and methodical way for appropriate results. In this study, case study methodology was adopted, which was part of the combined study undertaken for the objective "Leaping Beyond Vision" which is an intellectual human activity. It deals with techniques for gaining knowledge about the world by objectively investigating nature and matter. It deals particularly with the way data is collected, analysed, and interpreted (Pattron, 2009). The nature of the research problem primarily determines the way data can be collected, analysed, and interpreted. Methodology needs to be carefully selected, appropriate for the research situation and with an aim to understand the how and why of a phenomenon in its natural context (Yin, 2003).

Challenges & Need

Organisations are constantly challenged by the changing demands of the customers due to rapid changes in their business requirements. The changes in the business dynamics are creating challenges to meet the customer requirements. Therefore, it has become essential to understand these challenges and the need for undertaking this study. The challenges and needs are formulated in terms of objective and questions for an organised structured approach. The objective of this over all study was to explore and identify the factors responsible for success or failure of Indian marine projects in India. The study also explored the adequacy of the currently accepted criteria for measuring the performance and success of a project. To achieve the study objectives, the following questions were framed: -

a.   What are the project success criteria in marine projects and their role in project performance?

b.   What factors are responsible for the success and failure in Indian marine projects?

c.   How do these factors influence the project performance in Indian marine projects?

However, the main objective of this book (case studies) is to make all readers understand the cases in project management and how the dynamics in managing the project define success or failure of the project.

Technique

Hybrid Techniques were used for the study, the quantitative and qualitative approach. Strength of both the approaches were considered and combined for the analysis for this study. Brief on both the techniques are explained enabling the reader to understand the case studies from multidimensional perspective.

Qualitative approaches entail efforts to address the associated complexity involving the subjectivity in object of study which involves inherent bias ambiguity. As per this approach, the world is essentially relativistic thus, one should observe it from inside rather than outside by having first-hand knowledge and understanding of a phenomenon in conjunction with the applicable contextual variables. Such an effort generates in-depth, rich descriptions about the individuals and organisations by being sensitive to their ideas, processes and meanings (Denzin and Lincoln, 1994). This exercise may result in an empirically supported theory or model, which can be of considerable utility for practitioners.

Investigation Approach

To achieve the study objectives, the research framework for the investigation was evolved as indicated in the Figure 2.1. The study framework included exploratory (Stage 1) and descriptive (Stage 2) investigation approach based on Creswell, 2007, Eisenharldt, 2007 and Yin, 2003. In this book of case studies, the Stage two descriptive method is applicable, both the stages have been explained since the case studies being part of the overall study, which is described in the book "Leaping Beyond Vision"– final.

Exploratory Approach

Exploratory approach is selected with the objective to understand the unstated phenomenon underlying the shared experiences of the individuals, who are interacting with each other to achieve the same objectives. The research framework construed for the study is shown in the Figure 2.1. In Stage one, an interview was conducted through semi- structured questionnaire (personally administered) with the project practitioners to identify the critical tangible and intangible factors that affect the project performance. Data was collected from individuals who had experience in managing marine projects and were responsible for the project performance.

The unit of analysis in the interview is the individual project practitioners from the industry. Polkinghorne (1989) recommends that interview of 5 to 25 individuals who have experienced the phenomenon is adequate, yet 92 interviews were undertaken across the channel members with minimum five project practitioners from each channel member for "horizontalisation." The result from this study is used in understanding and validating the "why and how" (Yin, 2003) in the second stage by undertaking the case studies.

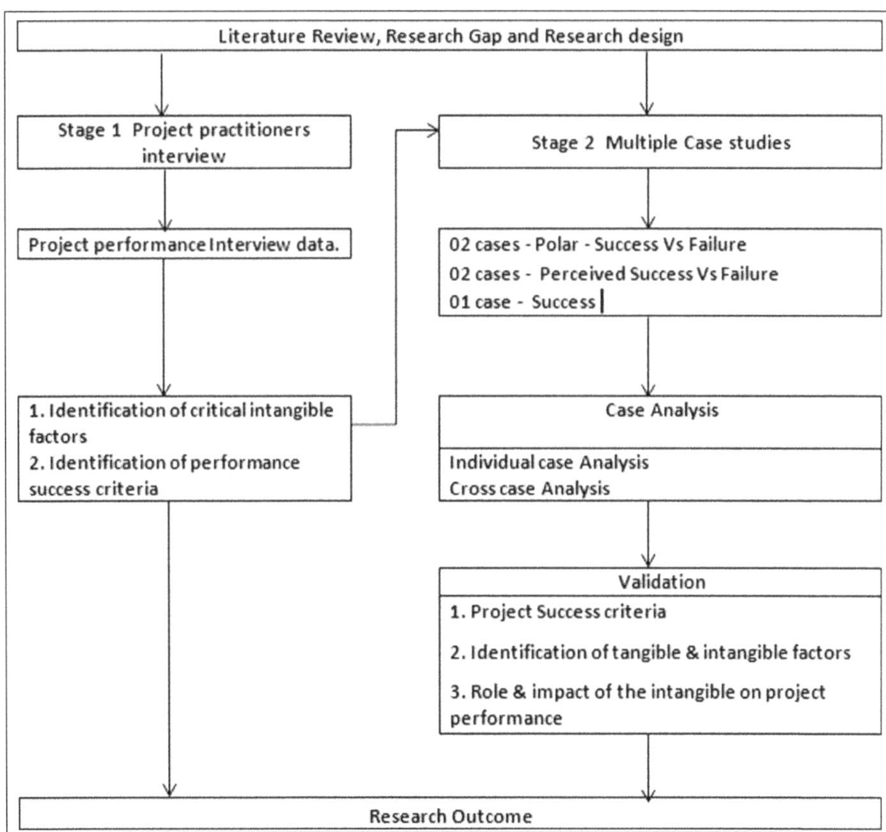

Figure 2.1: Research framework

Descriptive Approach

In the second stage, descriptive research approach is carried out through case study method with the objective to validate the identified factors, check the effects of identified factors and find additional factors, if any that affect the project performance? The case studies were considered to investigate a contemporary phenomenon within the real-life context, especially when boundaries between the phenomenon and the context are not clear. The present study has distinctive situations where more variables of interest are present than the data points and relies on multiple sources of evidence needing to converge for concrete results. A good understanding based on real-world experience can help tailor these techniques to specific project situations and develop a broader context of what works and what doesn't work in different situations.

Any theory based on multiple case studies that predicts dimensions and their relationships is expected to be deeply grounded and reliable, multiple cases help in ascertaining whether a finding is rare in a single case or replicated in different cases (Eisenhardt, 1991). Eisenhardt (1989) has prescribed 4 to 10 cases for theory building, which includes two steps: theory generation and testing. The theory evolved has been implemented in this study, which has given new dimension of validation, Ellram (1996) claims that a single case can be used to, "test a well-formulated theory, an extreme or unique case, or a case that represents a previously inaccessible phenomenon." Multiple cases, on the other hand, can help in replication leading to development of a rich theoretical framework (Ellram, 1996). Yin (1994) also recommended the use of two to three case studies for literal replication, hence the stages adopted is guided by Yin, (1994) as illustrated in Figure 2.2.

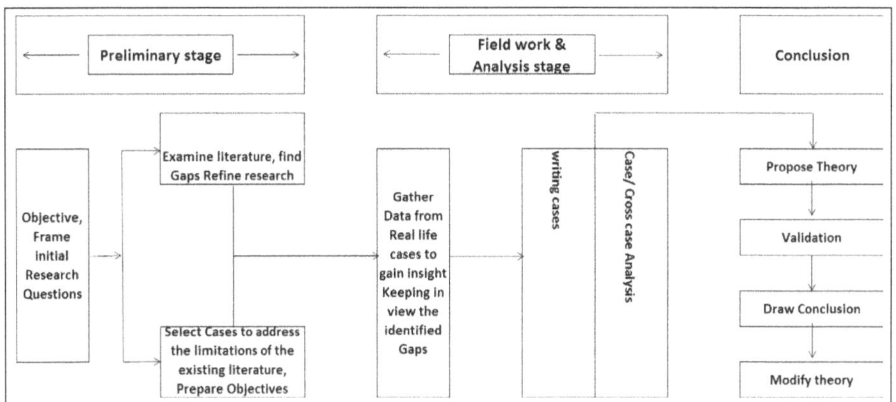

Figure 2.2: Typical stages in research Process (Yin, 1994)

Investigators select samples cases which have results opposite to each other as success or failure known as "polar types." This is done to provide a balanced representation to the samples in the population and to clearly discern the contrasting patterns in the data (Eisenhardt and Graebner, 2007). The cases in the sample may differ in terms of deliverables, however the approach towards managing the project has been considered. The cases selected for their differing results and the last case study corroborated the outcomes. The cases were selected from two different organisations to represent the oil & gas sector and shipbuilding sectors.

Case Selection

Cases have been selected such that the results can be applied to a wide range of similar situations. Related aspects for selection of such cases are population, sampling technique, and number of cases. Population refers to the set of entities from which relevant cases can be chosen. Population for the present study includes the cases in which projects were undertaken in the marine industry in the Indian context. Specifying what constitutes the population also helps in reducing extraneous variation (Eisenhardt, 1989).

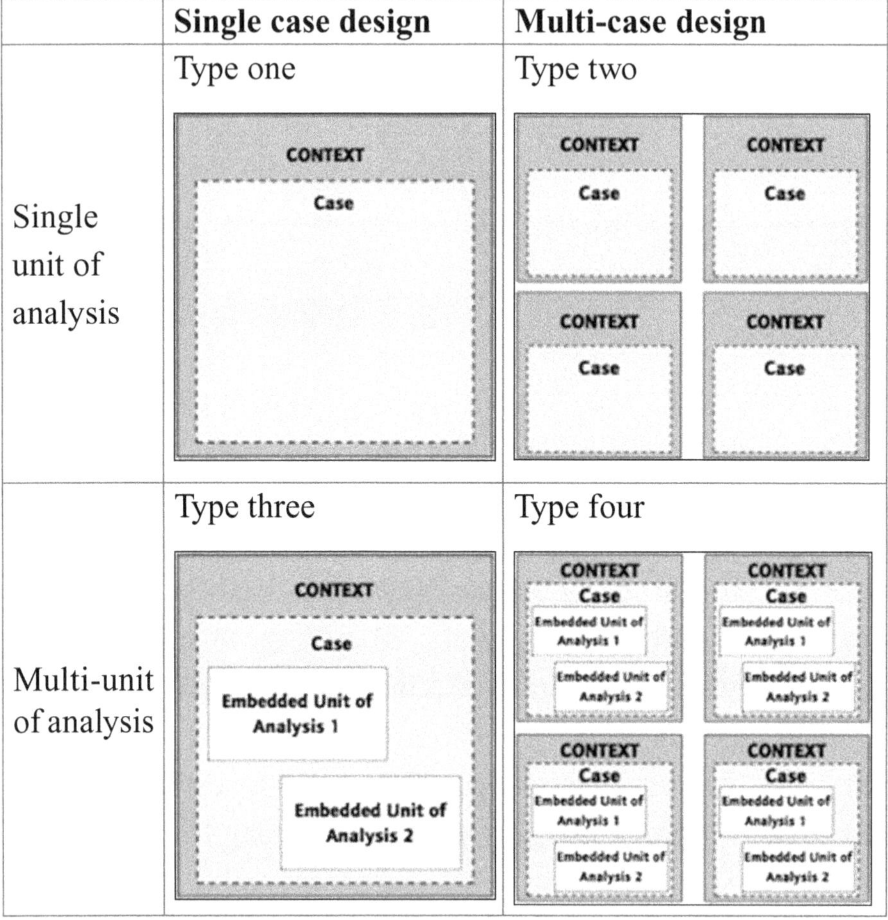

Figure 2.3: Function of Unit of Analysis and Case Designs (Yin, 1994)

Yin (1994) advised different possibilities for case studies as a function of the number of cases and the source of cases. Such possible combinations are shown in the Figure 2.3. In this study, it is planned to use case study of 'Type two' since a total of five case studies from two different organisations shall be used for generating and testing the theory. In other words, this study shall use five units of analysis from two sources. The project is the single unit of analysis in each case which is being evaluated within a multi-case design.

Data Collection

The data was collected through processed documents, archival records, interviews with project practitioners and observations. Process documents were studied to get an in-depth understanding of the procedures being followed. These included policy and procedures, inter and intra-project documentation, training provided to the project team, presentations given, test cases, communication plans, risk logs, status reports, outcome of retrospectives held, project tracking spreadsheets, release plans, pictures of white boards depicting outcome of discussions and weekly showcase presentations made by the project team to its customer.

Archival records of the organisation were also accessed for the purpose of cross- verification. These included a profile of team members, employee reference guide for clearer understanding of various processes, policy and project management practices and time sheet systems for confirmation of the effort put in by the team members on the project.

Interviews were carried out across the project channel organisations; an attempt was made to ensure that all roles in a team were represented. In the first instance, one person from each role was selected. Overall, 25-40 project practitioners were included for interview in the case studies, which included the sponsor, the project manager, project team members, procurement decision makers, commercial people dealing in payments and receivables, business controllers, sales team, project heads and others.

The duration of each interview was set to a maximum of one hour. In the first part of the interview, the selected candidates were given a background on the nature, scope and purpose of the study and the reasons for their selection. Their permission was sought in terms of whether they wanted to be a part of this study or not, and all the selected candidates chose to be associated with the study. Thereafter, they were asked questions related to their background and experience. The rest of the meeting was in the form of a discussion guide. Questions were focused around the research objective of the study and their experiences related to the same, benefits gained, and challenges faced from their perspective, and finally some of the differences in the practices followed in the particular project under discussion compared to other projects. The output from the discussions were transcribed and later confirmed with the participants to check whether they had been captured correctly.

Direct observations were carried out by visiting and meeting the people at site and assessing their on-site work behaviour. The observations were carried out to specifically identify motivational factors toward project practitioners such as the yard premise, office work space, the informal interaction within the team etc. Findings of such personal observations were taken as additional information for analysis.

Data Analysis and Interpretation

In qualitative research, data analysis is an ongoing process rather than a final stage (Miles and Huberman, 1994 Stake, 1995). Data collection and analyses were carried out concurrently. This made it possible to refine the data collection in line with the approach outlined by Creswell (1998). Data analysis followed the systematic approach described by Miles and Huberman (1994). It consisted of organising the data (i.e. the transcripts from interviews, and case data) for analysis and further reducing the data into themes through a process of coding and categorising, and finally representing the data in figures, tables, and discussions (Creswell, 1998). In the final book, cross case analysis along with the overall analysis is undertaken and concluded.

Case Studies

The discussion with the project interview was recorded in written format, the discussion was held with respect to the factors identified and to check the how these factors influence the project performance to success or failure. The new factors emerging from the discussions were reviewed, regrouped as a new major factor.

While developing the cases as well as while performing within case analysis the prime aim was to understand what success criteria approach was adopted and what factors influenced the project for its success or failure. With successive cases some new SFs also emerged. The researcher then went back to the previous cases and investigated the presence of the new SFs. Learning from each case was applied to collect, analyse and evaluate the data for subsequent cases. Thus, the data analysis in this study was an iterative process. In many instances the project practitioners were contacted again, and the secondary data revisited, to confirm or deny presence of specific factors in general as well as in specific cases.

The case was analysed within case analysis followed by cross case analysis (Yin, 2003). In addition, various factors which are mutually exclusive or inclusive or even independent of the system were analysed for their impact on the project success and considered for the theory building which are implementable in managing projects. The analysis of the study has been provided in the final book.

Five cases with differing results from Indian marine industry were selected. In each case around 25 to 40 project participants across the channel members were selected to participate in discussions to gather case-related primary data using discussion guide (provided in the final book). At the end of discussion, project participants were asked to rate each success factor for the influence on the iron triangle as success criteria. The average score of these factors is indicated and discussed in each case.

Secondary sources of data were collected from project documentation, policies and procedures, presentations, etc. made available by the participants. With a view to pursuing a pre-defined template for analysing case study data (Creswell, 1998), WCA was considered based on the approach adopted towards the completion of project deliverables. The criteria employed for case selection, data collection and sampling, case development, and data analysis and interpretation are detailed in the methodology chapter. A theoretical replication of the analytical procedures as suggested by Yin (2003) was adopted for the study.

The case study was undertaken to validate and check the adequacy of the success criteria and success factors identified in Stage one. Each case is evaluated based on the macro and micro WCA. The macro WCA was carried out based on the classification of the earlier studies on the project success. The micro WCA was carried out on the key success factors (tangible and intangible) identified in Stage one and is indicated in the final book. The projects in the cases have been evaluated as per the success criteria of the iron triangle since they are non-negotiable business requisites. Below sections provided the cases

Case A

Introduction

The ships are built in the shipyard's dry-dock, one of the dry-dock where the ship building is in progress as shown in the Figure 3.1.

Figure 3.1: Vessel in dry-dock

The case selected is a project from the marine sector which is Engineering, Procurement and management (EPM) turnkey type of contract. The project entailed detailed engineering, manufacturing, supply, and supervision of the equipment installation. The supply part involved, stern gear system (equipments present in the shaft line of a ship). The deliverable propulsion system by the OEM is shown in Figure 3.2 for understanding the scope of the project.

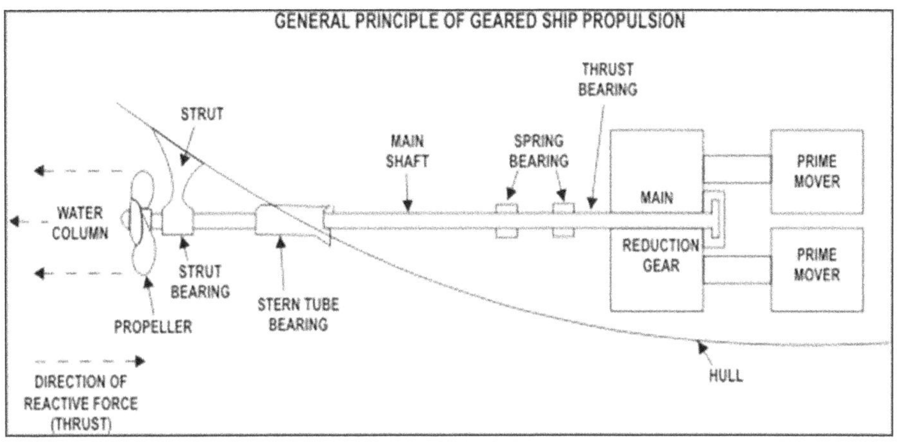

Figure 3.2: Propulsion system

The study was carried out on the main contractor, and across the channel members to understand factors that influenced the project outcome. The in-depth study was undertaken on the main contractor (yard) since they led the project for its outcome in this case. The key channel member consisted of end-user (Indian Navy), main contractor (Shipbuilder/ yard), Original Equipment Manufacturer (OEM), Vendors/ suppliers and sub-vendors/ sub-suppliers as shown in Figure 3.3.

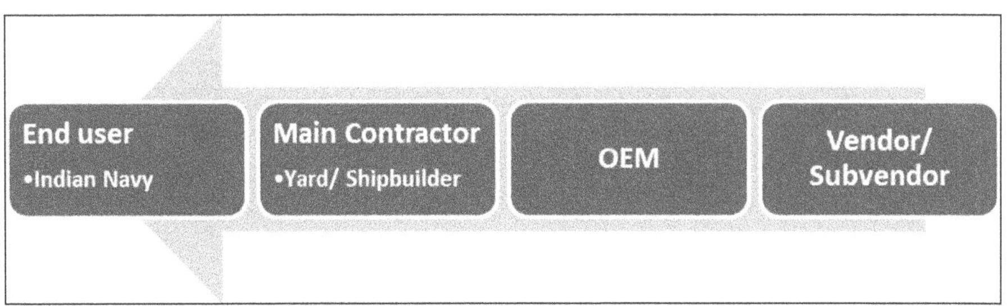

Figure 3.3: Case A - Channel Partners

Vendor & sub-vendor are those in the channel who provide either the raw material/ semifinished/ finished goods to the OEM which is used for the assembly of the OEM product directly or post value addition by the OEM. Most of the critical and technological activities involved in the manufacturing of the product were undertaken by the OEM. OEM was responsible for all the activities till installation commissioning, warranty, and post warranty services the life cycle of their product. Main contractor is one who is responsible for the delivery of the vessel to the owners and the end-user in the owner's organisation. Main contractor is the owner of the dry-dock, where the ships are built. They lay the keel of the ship and build the ship structures. Main contractor integrate all the systems and ensure that the vessel is ready to be handed over to the Owner/ User for its intended operations. They execute the whole programme of the vessel on behalf of the owners as a turnkey Project. Main contractor is the most critical part of the channel members, since they not only lead the programme but also integrate & control all the OEMs sub-contractors along with their teams. The end-user is at the highest level in the chain who places the order of the product (Vessel/ ship) on the main contractor for conversion of the need for the intended use. They give the basic high-level concepts with the required deliverable to the Main contractor and oversee the programme so that the deliverables are met as defined for the intended use. The brief of the channel members in this case is provided in the subsequent subsection.

Channel members

End-user

The end-user in this case is Indian Navy, which is the Naval branch of the armed forces of India. The President of India serves as the

Commander-in-Chief of the defence forces including Navy. The Chief of Naval Staff (CNS), is a four-star officer with rank of admiral, commands the Navy. Though the primary objective of the Navy is to secure national maritime interests, India also uses its Navy to enhance its international relations through joint exercises, port visits and humanitarian missions, including disaster relief.

India has a rich maritime history dating back 5000 years. The world's first tidal dock is believed to have been built at Lothal around 2300 BC during the Indus valley civilization, near the present day Mangrol harbour on the Gujarat coast. 17th century saw radical development in India under great Maratha emperor Chhatrapati Shivaji Maharaj, who is also considered as the 'Father of the Indian Navy in addition to the adaptation.' However modern Indian Navy inherited the legacy of Royal Indian Navy which was under the British Empire until India became independent in 1947. In recent years, the Indian Navy has undergone considerable modernisation by replacing ageing vessels in service and presently they are a fully-fledged Navy. To ensure the readiness of the operational fleet at all time with modernised ships and submarines, there is always the phasing out of the old and ageing ships and submarines with new and sophisticated ones. The acquisition of new ships and submarines has to undergo the tedious but robust and bureaucratic type of procurement process.

The defence procurements process in brief is, the contract for building the ship is awarded to qualified main contractors (shipbuilders /yards) based on least quote basis (L1) in their respective segments, however they have to procure the equipments for the ships from the qualified preferred vendor list who are mostly the OEM, else they have to get the vendors qualified for the supply of the material with the Naval specifications through the requisite qualification process. In this case, the vendor had to be a qualified OEM for the supply and installation of the stern gear system.

Main contractor

The main contractor (yard A) is in the marine shipbuilding industry for more than fifteen years with the experience of building various types of ships in varied segments of commercial ships. However, they were new entrant in the Naval segment and were qualified for lower tonnage non-warship vessels. The yard has full-fledged organisation for building ships, with a weak matrix (PMPBOK, 2017) type of OS. The OS is of the production type with human resources having technical expertise in their respective domain knowledge such as electrical, mechanical etc. however with less knowledge and experience in management roles. The organisation and project management in the case is illustrated at Figure 3.4.

OEM

OEM in this case is Wartsila (India), Wartsila (India) started its operation in the early eighties in India and has over twenty five years of experience in providing complete life-cycle power solutions for the Indian energy market. As a leading solutions provider of rapid and flexible power plants for Utilities industry, the name is now synonymous with decentralised energy market. They offer services, maintenance, and reconditioning solutions both for marine and power plants throughout the lifetime of the installations. Indian Navy, Coast Guard, Port Trusts, Merchant Shipping, floating cranes and offshore rigs.

Wartsila (India) is 100% subsidiary of Wartsila (Finland), the organisation is divided into three business areas – Ship power, Power plant and services. The business areas are supported by Wartsila Industrial operations, and other support functions such as finance and control, supply chain, human resource, information management, legal etc.

Wartsila are global leader in complete life-cycle power solutions for the marine and energy markets. By emphasising technological innovation and total efficiency, Wartsila maximises the environmental and economic performance of the vessels and power plants of its customers. The company has operations in 160 locations in seventy countries around the world with 18,000 employees (approximately).

Project Management Brief

The case study was undertaken with the project participants on the basis of the discussion guide across the project channel with focus on the main contractor (yard /shipbuilder). Main contractor also known as shipbuilder, is the main engineering and construction (E&C) contractor, responsible for the delivery of the vessel. The scope of the project was to supply and commission the stern gear system as per the agreed contract. The stern gear system is a critical part of the vessel being built by the E &C contractor. The project details of the case are indicated in Table 3.1.

In this case, the main contractor accepted the OEM reluctantly due to pressure from the end-user, even the end-user based on the

Table 3.1: Case A - Project details

S.No	Criteria	Data/Information	Remarks
1	Scope	Supply & commissioning of equipment (Stern gear system)	Fixed - however increased without cost and schedule impact
2	Cost	2.57 crores	Fixed (51.5 lakhs/shipset) for five shipsets
3	Time (project duration)	08 month for 1st Shipset 10 months for 2nd & 3rd shipset 12 month for last two shipset	Contractual terms - project duration to commence from release of PO and advance. LOI provided, however PO and advance payment delayed by two weeks and by 07 weeks respectively. Delivery dates not changed
4	Contract type	EPM – Engineering Procurement and management (Installation & commissioning supervision)	OEM expertise also used for design related issues
5	Organisation's structure (OS)	Functional (Kerzner, 2013, PMBOK, 2008)	The OS restricted the PM functions there by affecting the project execution for the desired success criteria
6	Channel members	Four(including OEM)	Engg consultant not considered part of the team during project execution along with other stakeholder.

main contractor risk analysis had regretted the RFQ. However end-user insisted the OEM to take up the contract. The main contractor was keen to qualify a new vendor as OEM for the turnkey Project, but the end-user was unwilling to deviate from the qualified OEM's. Therefore, conflicts of interest existed prior and during contract formulation, this being the major reason for the project lacking a cooperative and collaborative approach. In addition, OEM had shown reluctance to work with the main contractor due to the lower rating results obtained during customer and stakeholder analysis. Nevertheless, OEM accepted the project on end-user's request at the low price negotiated by main contractor. This had inflicted an element of unwillingness on the part of both, main contractor as well as OEM to work together and induced distrust among the project participants and the channel members. Main Contractor, despite being a new entrant into the defence industry, focused on cost as the success criteria and gave lesser importance on the time, scope and mainly quality. The communication was limited and formal wherein, most of the issues were escalated to the main contractor top management. Therefore, end-user and OEM had to manage most of the non-scope related activities to ensure that the project met the scope and time criteria. This had induced hesitation among the project participants towards forming any cooperative and collaborative approach. project participants and channel members were more interested in safeguarding their localised organisational and personal interest. The main contractor had set-up a functional type of organisation structure (Kerzner, 2013, Cleland, 1999, Gary and Larson, 2000, Meredith and Mantel, 2000, PMBOK, 2008) for the project management dynamics and organisation structure controlling the activities are indicated in Figure 3.4. The nominated project manager was at a lower level, with limited PM skillsets and empowerment. An autocratic and top-down decision-making style from top management to the middle management was evident in all the project related activities. Most decisions were skewed towards the cost parameter, which led to a negative impact on the overall project performance.

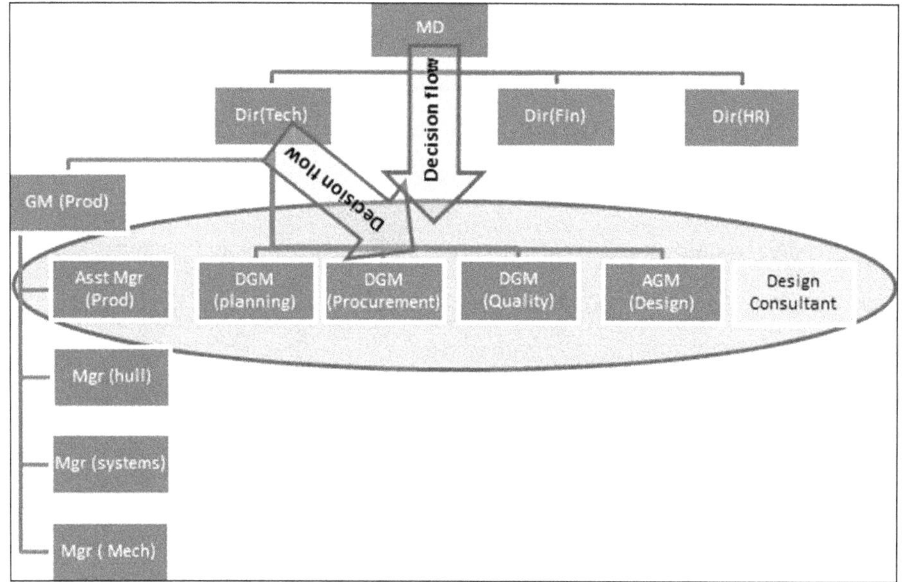

Figure 3.4: Case A - Project organisation and management

Despite being a new entrant, the main contractor did not give due importance to stakeholder analysis and instead concentrated on the client's specification and policy-related requirement which was necessary to be adhered to for the deliverables. This has led to inter and intra-organisation conflicts, and delay in the project schedule. The Table 3.2 summarises the project management details.

Table 3.2: Case A - Project management details

S.No	Criteria	Data/Information	Remarks
1	Project manager skills	Lower-level in the OS and inexperienced in PM	Project could not be managed by the project manager hence affected the project performance
2	Communication	Low and formal	Only formal communications
3	Channel partners Relationship	Poor - Inter & Intra-conflicts (main contractor) very high	Main contractor did not entertain any formal or informal request. project related technical clarification to stake holders not in the scope had to be attended by OEM
4	Stakeholders - management	Stake holder analysis not undertaken and minimal management	As new entrant into the segment stake holder analysis and management is critical hence caused uncertainty and confusions during execution which impacted the project success
5	Decision-Making	Centralised - Controlled by top management. project team - Less empowered.	The project coordinator had to refer back to either technical or managing director for issue resolution

Project Execution

The contract negotiation was held between yard and OEM representatives as per the process defined by the end-user for

OEM selection. Though the contract negotiation needs to be held between the yard and OEM for project commencement. However, the end-user had to intervene as the stern gear system delivery package was getting delayed due to yard's insistence to approve a new vendor for the system. The main reason for the introduction of a new vendor was to lower the work package (contract value) cost. The end-user therefore intervened and initiated the contract negotiation between the yard and the OEM. The contract negotiation was more on the cost side than technical, scope, or other terms and conditions. Despite OEM's rating, based on the customer analysis of the yard (being the customer) as high-risk from commercial, schedule and reputation attribute they accepted the contract offered by yard. The reason being, Indian Navy (end-user) is an esteemed and important customer for OEM and OEM had good reputation with high rating as a qualified vendor. Therefore, it is observed that in the initial phase the project experienced conflicts and low degree of trust between the OEM and yard.

Post award of the project as contract, the advance was released seven weeks late against the contract agreement (PO). There was no formal kick off between the OEM and yard, however it was informed by the yard that a project coordinator was appointed to oversee this Project. The assigned project coordinator was at a lower level in the OS. During project execution the coordinator was changed four times due to various reasons. For all technical and managerial related issues with the end-user, coordinator had to seek support from other project channel members which otherwise was yards responsibility. The yard always kept the authority, however held responsible the respective project channel member participant. In the early stage (design), the engineering inputs were not acknowledged and accepted from the appointed consultant, leading to inadequate adherence to the requirements of the classification agency. This caused a delay during the initial approval stage, against planned duration thereby causing cascading effect to the subsequent activities.

During the execution phase of the project, the end-user identified that yard had not included few required system equipments in the scope as deliverables. Yard, therefore insisted OEM to include in the scope without any additional cost or time. Few minor deviations were accepted, however major deviations were not accepted, hence OEM had to provide the technical specifications and designs for the equipments (not in scope), enabling the main contractor to be procured directly. Since the yard had not accepted consultant's suggestions, prior to approval of drawings there were several changes in the specifications. This also caused disruption in the execution phase as few of the activities were undertaken based on the initial approval provided by the yard with anticipation that same would have no effects on the end-user approval.

Though the yard project team members were skilled and capable, they were reluctant to provide the necessary decision. They either diverted the issues or requested escalation. The reason being, all the decisions had to be routed through their directors, as most of the decisions were taken by the top management and the decisions usually were cost or scope oriented. The schedule and quality related matters were not given priority and were meant to be resolved by the project coordinator. The coordinator, being at a lower level, did not have adequate empowerment and authority over the other departments; therefore, things were not under his control. Further the OS being a weak matrix disallowed proper integration of the departments to work towards common objective.

In this case the yard was responsible and detrimental to the project performance, since they being the only decision maker, the decision-making was affecting the project activities across the channel partners. The interaction between the OEM and yard team were of formal type with fewer interactions, since the decision-making capacity vested with the top management, this incapacitated the team members from taking any decisions and demotivated them. This type of decision-making disallowed other project participants to take any initiatives towards the project. Therefore during the execution of project, the project endured with many technical, managerial and contractual related issues. The resolution of the issues raised or evolved took excessive time due to several iteration of discussions between yard, OEM designer and end customer to agree upon common consensus. The locus of control with respect to decision-making was held by the yard, which was based on the cost and scope alone so that any cost escalation could be curtailed to maximum. There were additions to the scope of supply, without extra cost to OEMs, few were accepted by OEM and others not accepted remained a sore point as yard had to procure the same. The absence of proper a communication process had caused confusions within the project environment and the channel members. In addition, the change in the project coordinator caused delay in understanding and adaptation to the project, one of the major reasons for change was attrition.

The channel members after experiencing the devoid of participative approach towards the project objective, changed their strategy and focused towards their interest of the tangible factor such as cost and scope. This made the channel member apprehensive about the project viability as the yard did not give adequate attention towards the schedule and the project was getting delayed beyond reasonable limit. Since the project was getting delayed, the OEM focused towards the documentations that would disallow yard to levy liquidated damages (LD). This made the project achieve lower project performance, as there were wide deviations with regards to the project success criteria "Iron triangle."

On discussion with the project participants with regards to the macro factors, most of the project participant agreed that they considered the cost and scope as success criteria since these factors affected the project budgets. The lack of cooperative and collaborative approach inter & intra-organisation disallowed any positive interplay of intangible factors which is necessary for a project to be successful. The yard project team members were distributed in three different locations, which also caused communication related issues, and this was also one of the contributors towards the project delay. The external environment did not have any impact on the project performance, however in contrast the internal environment had severe effect on the project results. Team members informed that there were no differentiations in approach towards managing the project, all projects were treated the same. They carried out activities as directed by their supervisors or directives of top management. It was also indicated that they preferred empowerment and decision-making authority at their level and domain. Therefore, they desired changes in the present organisation culture, which needs to be more transparent and integrating with other departments. The change suggested would enable them to be more informed about the work being undertaken and align their efforts towards a common goal. Most of the project participants were unaware of the end-user objective and few were ignorant about the organisation strategic decision for the new order. The individual performance was rated as per the departments set goals, which made the departments compete with each other thereby creating non-cooperative approach.

The team acknowledged the absence of the required intangible factors which could have enhanced the project performance. The project coordinator lacked the requisite skills and experience that is necessary to execute any project. The motivation was low within the team members, and this was reflected by the attrition rate. Stakeholder analysis is critical and same was not undertaken by the yard, in addition their project requirements were also not understood and attended appropriately. Nevertheless, OEM in this case ensured that the project related requirements were attended and reported appropriately to the end-user.

The project was a failure from the iron triangle perspective, as it had exceeded the time and cost success criteria. In addition, the stake holders, mainly end-user, project participants and other channel members view it as a failure. The failure was attributed to the absence of the right intangibles, due to which the objectives were not met and even the project participants were disappointed. A detailed analysis of the WCA of the case is provided in the final book.

Case B

Introduction

Case B is similar to Case A, however a successful project there by making it polar to the Case A. The contract type and deliverable remained same; however, deliverables also included supply of Sewage Treatment Plant (STP) as shown in Figure 3.5, and its integration with the vessels systems.

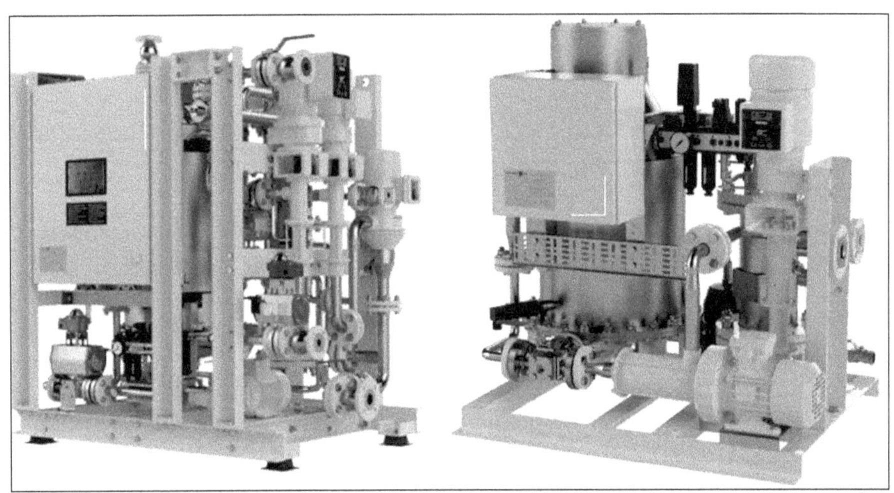

Figure 3.5: Sewage treatment plant (STP)

The selected project is also a marine; Engineering, EPM turnkey type of contract. The project entailed detailed engineering, manufacturing, supply, and supervision of the equipment installation. The supply part entailed a stern gear system as supplied in Case A. In this case also an in-depth study was carried out on the main contractor since the main contractor was responsible for the project outcome along with the channel members.

The channel members in this case are, end-user (Indian Navy), main contractor (Shipbuilder/ yard), OEM, Vendors / supplier and Sub-vendors / sub-suppliers remained same as described in the Case A, except for the main contractor as shown in Figure 3.6.

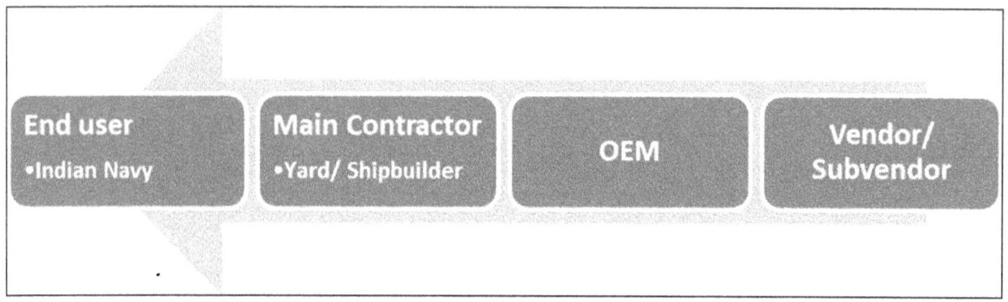

Figure 3.6: Case B - Channel partners

Channel Members

End-user

The end-user remained the same as in Case A. The case was selected intentionally so that the sensitivity of the dynamics is checked based on change of only one attribute.

Main Contractor

The main contractor (yard B) is in the marine shipbuilding industry for more than ten years with the experience of building various types of ships in varied segments of commercial ships. However, they were also new entrant in the Naval segment and were qualified for lower tonnage non-warship vessels. Main contractor had a lean OS, with very few project team members for building ships and similar a modified projectised matrix (PMPBOK, 2017). The organisation is headed by one of the directors supported by a nominated project manager for each class of ships, in turn project manager is supported by team members as per the ship's origination structure viz hull (ship structure), engineering, electrical and other auxiliaries. The organisation and project management in the case is illustrated in Figure 3.7.

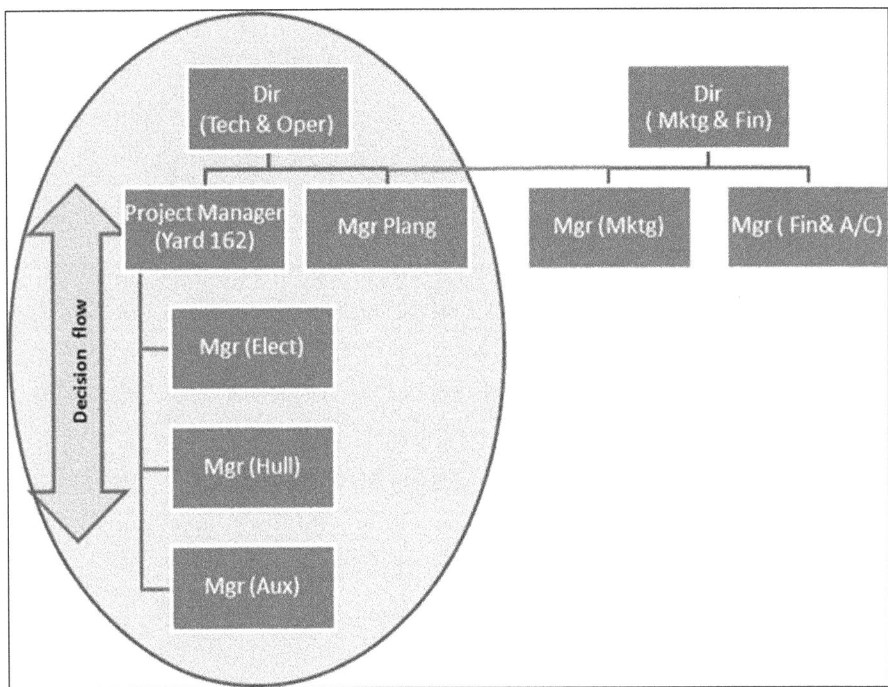

Figure 3.7: Case B - Project organisation and management

OEM

Case A OEM remained same in the Case B.

Project Management Brief

Similar to Case A, shipbuilder (main contractor) was responsible for the project outcome hence the study was undertaken with main contractor being the epicentre for the analysis. The project details are as provided in the Table 3.3.

In contrast to Case A, the main contractor in Case B had unintentionally focused on building relationships with the project participants across the channel members. Main contractor and OEM had pre-bid meetings and proper negotiations for the contract. This very process brought into play several positive intangible factors such as high trust among project participants across channel members, motivated team, innovative approach, empowerment into the project environment along with the tangible factors. Initial contracting experience had encouraged the channel members and the project participants to be more risk taking, hence they were innovative.

Cooperative and alliance type of organisational set-up of the project team, helped the project in achieving its objectives.

Table 3.3: Case B - Project details

S.No	Criteria	Data/Information	Remarks
1	Scope	Supply & commissioning of equipment (Stern gear system) and STP	Fixed
2	Cost	1.26 crores (90 Lakhs for stern gear system)	Fixed (60 lakhs/shipset) for two shipsets. 3 lakhs/ shipset (20%) provided additional for the STP since wrong estimation by OEM

S.No	Criteria	Data/Information	Remarks
3	Time (project duration)	08 month for both shipset	Contractual terms - PO and advance released in time
4	Contract type	EPM – Engineering Procurement and management (Installation & commissioning supervision)	OEM expertise used for related design issues as required by end-user
5	Organisation structure (OS)	Strong matrix (Kerzner, 2013, PMBOK, 2008), with lean team	OS enhanced the authority of the project manager, hence better resolution of issues.
6	Channel members	Four (including OEM)	Engg consultant was directly handled by main contractor

The contract only mentioned iron triangle as the project objective, but the main contractor had encouraged end-user satisfaction with respect to functional requirements. The focus was to ensure that all the stakeholders and the channel members were in agreement with the end-user's requirements.

In this case, the top management empowered project participants to take decisions in alignment with project objectives. The project OS was of lean and strong matrix type, under control of an experienced project manager with relevant skills. The PM activities that encompassed this project are shown in the Figure 3.7.

Further, a collaborative and participative approach was adopted towards all project participants while critical decisions were taken by the main contractor. The project management details are provided in Table 3.4.

Table 3.4: Case B - Project management details

S.No	Criteria	Data/Information	Remarks
1	project manager skills	Experienced and skilled in PM	project was effectively managed, thus leading to project success
2	Communication	Adequate, formal, and informal	Communication was key to the project success as all stakeholders were appropriately informed.
3	Channel partners Relationship	Alliance	The issue resolution by participation did not allow any conflicts and created better relationship
4	Stakeholders - management	The interests of the stake holder were considered till commissioning.	Stakeholder analysis undertaken by main contractor prior to acceptance of vessel contract. Minor scope changes accepted without extra cost
5	Decision- Making	Participative with channel partners	The project manager & team empowered to take decisions in their capacity

Project Execution

As per the process, the contract negotiation was held between main contractor (yard) and OEM representative. The contract negotiation was held in a formal manner, however with an informal approach along with required team members and the yard directors. Directors were present to ensure that the contract is finalised and accepted on the same day. The negotiations between the main contractor and OEM mainly focused on ensuring that the scope is well understood from the end-user perspective with time being the governing factor. The initial experience of contract finalisation set-up the cooperative environment of project alliance thus making means for accepting and resolving any future issues and challenges in mutual way.

Post award of the project as contract, the advance was released within one week. A formal kick off between OEM and yard was held with their respective team members participating in the meeting. Yard appointed a project manager, who was responsible for the entire vessel including the subject Project. All team members of the project were located at one place to enable better interaction within the team and decisions are taken without any delay. The team members were highly empowered hence most of the issues which emanated were resolved very fast, critical issues if any were escalated to appropriate authority. The formal communication process was formulated for inter and intra-organisation, nevertheless most of the interaction was informal and the same was extended to the external project participants.

In the early stage (design), the engineering inputs were verified and accepted from the appointed consultant, and then put up for the necessary approval which was in accordance to the required specifications of the classification agency. The project team of yard B took very less support from the end customers with respect to the project execution requirements. They maintained a good communication channel, formal and informal for the project status reporting and information. The project manager was constantly in communication with all stakeholders for ensuring the project meets the success criteria and was well supported by the team members. The project manager was an experienced person at mid-level in the OS, and well versed with the managerial skill necessary for the project management.

In this case yard used to collate necessary issues or clarifications from all channel members and accordingly updated end-user in fortnightly meeting. This type of interaction and communication helped in anticipation and resolution of the issues appropriately in time. The yard B organisation respected other project channel members and hence took the decisions by participative method.

During execution, the project was confronted with various issues; however same were resolved with cooperative approach and with mutual agreement on risk if any. The focus was on relationship and trust as the centre of locus yet giving equal importance to the schedule and quality of the project. There were very few design changes, as adequate time was given in understanding the project specification and channel member's requirements during the planning phase. In one of the instances, post acceptance of the contract OEM submitted that, error had occurred in their estimation, therefore keeping trust in the OEM submission, they increased the value such that OEM were break-even for their project. The project saw a few innovative ways of resolving the challenges confronted, and same were shared across the channel members as knowledge sharing process for future adaptability.

The project manager had a good leadership traits and he remained constant throughout the project completion. The team members were empowered to take decisions in their capacity and were supportive to the project manager, only one team member left the team during project execution phase. On analysis from the observations, interview, and documentations, it was inferred that the project had excellent cooperative environment which complemented the team member's motivation. The team was cohesive with healthy interaction both, inter and intra-organisation.

Yard in this case was the facilitator for the positive environment, they considered the intangible factors unintentionally, and thereby ensuring symbiotic way of working is established across the channel members. Though importance was given to the intangible factors, prime focus was on the schedule and quality since they were crucial project success criteria.

On discussion with project participants with regards to the macro factors, most of the project participant confirmed that end-user satisfaction and project objectives considered was the key to positive project results. The schedule and quality were considered as the prime success criteria along with the end-user satisfaction and project objectives which influenced the project to be successful. The cooperative and collaborative approaches, inter and intra-organisation enabled positive interplay of tangible and intangible factors which also played critical role in the success of project. The project team was located at one place, which enabled better communications, thus aiding to faster decision-making and issue resolution. The external environment did not have any impact on the project performance, but the internal environment influenced the project performance due to positive interplay of the intangible factors for constructive effect. Team members informed that there were no differentiations in approach towards managing the project, and all projects were treated as same. The team members were empowered to take decisions in the interest of the project and organisation. This helped the team members in converging their efforts towards common the project objectives.

The team acknowledged the presence of intangible factors which enhanced the project performance. The project manager played a vital role in the integration of the organisation and key stakeholders. Yard had undertaken the stakeholder analysis and especially of the end-user so that their needs are well understood from project perspective and are attended appropriately during project execution.

This was a successful project from the iron triangle perspective, as the cost and quality success criteria were achieved. The schedule of the project deviated by one month, as it was minor deviation and did not affect the yard and end-user schedule, hence was acceptable therefore it was still considered a success from schedule criterion also. In addition, the stakeholders, end-user, project participants and other channel members perceived the project as successful. The success of the project was attributed to presence of the right intangible factors, due to which the project objectives were met along with the tangible success criteria.

The performance of the project was much above the specified performance parameters of iron triangle as well as the intangible factors. This project success gave better rewards such as orders for building for additional ships of same class as well as other class. Partnership, Memorandum of understanding for building ships with key channel members was agreed upon and signed. The specification and WCA details of the case are given in the final book.

Case C

Cases C is selected from the newly built projects in the oil & gas sector for generalisation across the marine industry. The project presented as Case C is also EPM type for supply of pedestal type American API monogrammed crane. The scope entailed engineering, manufacturing, testing at factory known as Factory acceptance test (FAT), installation supervision at platform and conducting the Site acceptance test (SAT).

Introduction

This case study was carried out on a project selected from an oil and gas sector, segment of marine industry. The project considered is an EPM type, which entailed engineering, manufacturing, testing at factory known FAT and supervision of installation at platform, conducting the site acceptance test SAT, and management of equipment installation. The project entailed supply of the pedestal type American API monogrammed crane. The project channel members were viz., end customer Oil and Natural Gas Corporation Ltd. (ONGC), main contractor (EPCI contractor), OEM, vendors/ supplier, and the sub-vendors/ sub-supplier, same is shown at Figure 3.8.

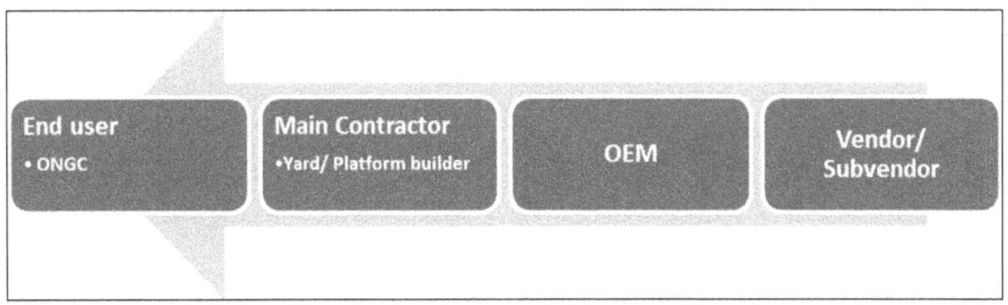

Figure 3.8: Case C - Channel partners

The subsequent subsections provide the brief on the channel members and project execution brief.

Channel Members

End-user

The end-user is Oil and Natural Gas Corporation Ltd. (ONGC). ONGC was set-up under the visionary leadership of Pandit Jawahar Lal Nehru. The foundation was laid as ONGC in the form of oil and gas division, under Geological Survey of India, in 1955. A few months later, it was converted into an Oil and Natural Gas Directorate. The Directorate was converted into commission and christened Oil and Natural Gas commission on 14th August 1956. In 1994, Oil and Natural Gas commission was converted into a corporation, and in 1997 it was recognised as one of the 'Navratnas' by the Government of India. Subsequently, it has been conferred with 'Maharatna' status in the year 2010.

Over fifty years of its existence ONGC has crossed many milestones. Today, ONGC is the leader in Exploration and Production (E&P) activities in India having 72% contribution to India's total production of crude oil and 48% of natural gas. ONGC has established more than seven billion Tons of in-place hydrocarbon reserves in the country. In fact, six out of seven producing basins in India have been discovered by ONGC. ONGC produces more than 1.27 million Barrels of Oil Equivalent (BOE) per day. It also contributes over three million tons per annum of Value-Added-Products including LPG, C2 - C3, Naphtha, MS, HSD, Aviation Fuel, SKO etc.

Main Contractor

The main contractor is the largest owner and operator of offshore support vessels in Malaysia and is an established and trusted service partner in the oil and gas industry. They have established a strong position in FPSO systems, a growing transport and installation business and competency in the management of large projects. They currently serve clients in southeast Asia, Congo, India, Mexico, Africa, Venezuela and the Caspian Sea region.

The company was incorporated in December 1995 as a public limited company (under the Companies Act, 1965), and the group of companies includes diversified subsidiaries as well as joint venture companies. Contractor C is a matured with advanced organisation for building the oil and gas platforms, organisation structure present can be called as strong projectised matrix (main contractor). The project in this case was being coordinated and managed by project coordinator. However the responsibility laid on the procurement department for expediting and resolution of issues related to turnkey type of sub-project for building the platform.

OEM

G &T Oil States Industries Pvt. Ltd (GTOSI) is the OEM in this case. Oil States (Asia) Pte. Ltd, Singapore is a wholly owned subsidiary of Oil States Industries, Inc.-USA, with joint venture with G & T Oilfield Offshore services Pvt. Ltd., set-up G & Oil States Industries Pvt. Ltd GTOSI. They were therefore qualified to, design (under JVP), manufacture, supply and provide after-sales support for all models of Nautilus make offshore cranes, all models of Patriot make offshore cranes covered under the Patriot technology license agreement (Patriot cranes installed and / or in service with ONGC and others in the Indian waters), and modular offshore cranes including rental contracts on turnkey basis.

Oil States International, Inc. is a diversified solutions provider for the oil and gas industry. With locations around the world, Oil States is a leading manufacturer of capital equipment for deep water production facilities and subsea pipelines, and a leading service provider to the oil and gas industry, including remote site accommodations, production-related rental tools, oil country tubular goods distribution and land drilling services. Oil States is publicly traded on the New York Stock Exchange under the symbol OIS. All the operations of the GTOSI are governed and guided by Oil States Industries Ltd Houma as per the JV technology transfer for building the cranes.

GTOSI started the operations in mid-2010 and the project considered in the case was received in Dec 2011. The organisation was weak matrix initially when the project commenced. The organisation is headed by the Managing Director (MD) and supported by Chief Operating Officer (COO) who also joined the organisation in the mid of the project execution phase. COO was assisted by Chief financial Officer, head of departments, viz, Engineering, Procurement, Production, Quality, project and other supporting functions HR, Admin, and Accounts.

Project Management Brief

The discussion guide was used for conducting the case study across the project channel participants with focus on the OEM.

The project management approach by the OEM defined the project result. The main contractor (EPCI contractor) is the platform builder who is responsible for the delivery of the platform where the crane is being installed. The objective of the project was to supply and commission the crane as per the agreed contract. As per the requirements of the guidelines, the crane is a critical structure on the platform for material lifting and personnel lifts (whenever necessary) on board. The project details of the case are indicated in Table 3.5.

Table 3.5: Case C - Project details

S.No	Criteria	Data/Information	Remarks
1	Scope	Design, manufacture, supply and commissioning of API monogrammed Crane	Fixed
2	Cost	9.75 Crores (02 cranes)	Fixed (4.87 Crore/ crane)
3	Time (duration)	08 and 08 -1/2 months respectively	Fixed
4	Contract type	EPM – Engineering Procurement, management (Installation & commissioning supervision)	Turnkey type – Cost of management additional
5	Organisation structure	Weak matrix (Kerzner, 2013, PMBOK, 2008)	OS restricted the PM functions and coordination. Confusion over the reporting and the objectives. Affected the project execution for the desired success criteria

S.No	Criteria	Data/Information	Remarks
6	Immediate customer	Main contractor	For first time the OEM was handling EPCI type contractor hence had lot of project related issues
7	Channel members	Four(including OEM)	Direct order , hence lesser levels

In this case, lack of cooperation within and between departments in the organisation was easily discerned. The existence of both formal and informal organisation structures in the OEM had created confusions within the organisation. Therefore, project participants were focused towards personal, departmental, and sub-organisational goals. The project management activities were controlled directly by the Managing Director of the OEM at department head level as indicated in Figure 3.9. The project decisions were influenced based on the cost and scope.

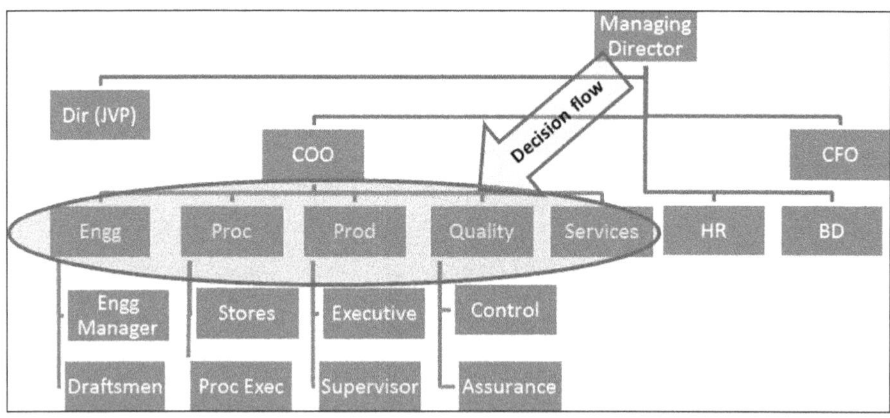

Figure 3.9: Case C - Project organisation and management

Conflicts existed since conception of the project, as the OEM and JVP had conflicting objectives, due to which project participants were confused. Being a recent startup, the OEM acted independently without consideration of experienced JVP and agreed to supply six cranes in one year, whereas their past experience has been restricted to supply of one crane in a year. The project management details of the case are as shown in Table 3.6.

Table 3.6: Case C - Project management details

S.No	Criteria	Data/Information	Remarks
1	Project manager skills	Higher level in OS but inexperienced in PM	Project could not be managed by the project manager hence affected the project performance
2	Communication	High and formal	High but only formal communications
3	Channel partners Relationship	Poor	Strained with all channel members.
4	Stakeholders - management	Stake holder analysis not undertaken and minimal management	As new entrant into the Indian industry stake holder analysis and management is critical. Focus was more on cost savings than commitment towards the schedule.
5	Decision-Making	Centralised - Controlled by top management in OEM Organisation	Decision-making, and some time was not an informed decision – Autocratic type

Project Execution

The project negotiation for the contract was held between the procurement and project team of the contractors and MD with sales head from OEM. The negotiation of the project was smooth however the contract was awarded to OEM (technically qualified since JV) only on commitment towards adherence to the negotiated schedule which was to be formulated into the contract. The negotiation process did not have any significant issues, and most of the terms were accepted by the OEM in urgency for the requirement of independent order. In this case the OEM had the direct order and joint venture partner were not part of the channel.

Since the beginning of the project, poor cash flow and indecisive decision-making were weakening trust inter and intra-organisation. Non-payment of fees payable to channel partners, had further strained the relationship. Motivation of project participants in the OEM organisation was low due to the huge variation in the resource requirement, job insecurity among employees, and the master-servant type relationship between the management and workers. The project management details of the case are as shown in Table 3.7.

The project was also delayed due to another unlikely reason was grand opening of the new facility. The assembly and testing of the crane was to be undertaken at new facility, however the same got delayed since the opening of the facility got extended for want of appropriate chief guest; hence all the resources were diverted causing a delay of 25 days. Most of the stakeholders, including the main contractor and the end-user, were unhappy with the reasons for the delay.

A significant amount of the project funds was also diverted towards the opening ceremony, there by affecting the cash flow required for the timely completion of the project .

Since the beginning of the project, poor cash flow and indecisive decision-making were weakening trust inter and intra-organisation. Non-payment of fees payable to channel partners, had further strained the relationship. Motivation of project participants in the OEM organisation was low due to the huge variation in the resource requirement, job insecurity among employees, and the master-servant type relationship between the management and workers.

OEM had a weak OS (PMPBOK, 2017) with design head nominated as project manager. Nominated project manager was an expert in the design activities and did not have any experience in the project management. The project initiations was undertaken by handing over of project to the project manager in an internal meeting, known as internal contract review and with release of internal work order. The internal work order is a document which defines the project scope in detail, so that whenever internal participants have any ambiguity, they can refer to this document for clarity. However in this project the document was incomplete with open ended statements. The schedule of the project was based on the purchase order with a fixed date, the micro level schedule in Microsoft project (MSP) was prepared by JVP and provided to the project manager, since there was no expertise in MSP, and the schedule provided was not tracked, hence became redundant. The role for the project manager was not well-defined hence the same was limited only to status reporting to customer and communication for the same. The budget was not provided to project manager hence the same was neither tracked nor controlled by the project manager. The projects were reviewed weekly directly by MD for most of the project phase, prior to handing it over to COO (in the last phase of project). The team also had reporting to their functional counter parts at Oil States Skagit Smatco (OSSS) Houma, this included participation in the virtual weekly meetings for project progress review. Despite handing over to COO, the decision-making vested with MD, a Centralised type decision-making structure. The project was internally coordinated at department heads level; since the roles were also not clearly defined it had caused confusions within the team.

The engineering phase of the project was prolonged due to the approval process, since OEM had to take approvals from the JVP, as the design capability was available only with them. The procurement department, apart from the procurement, vendor development, vendor liaising, expediting, import/ export, customs and excise activities was also responsible of the stores, receipt and dispatch materials of the entire crane in knock down condition (disassembled state).

The participants involved in the procurement are engineering, quality, production department and OEM corporate office, from JVP, design, procurement, and project department. In addition to these departments, the imports were to be routed through OEM London office, which handled the activities from enquiry generation to shipment of the item.

The procurement in this case was being undertaken by two different methods, imports and domestic. In imports, the list of items was provided by the JVP, and rest of the activities was controlled by import coordinator under the supervision of MD corporate office at Delhi to keep the cost confidential. Since the project was directly placed by main contractor on OEM, therefore the responsibility of ensuring the project is executed and completed in all aspect was on OEM. However the specifications for these materials were available only with JVP and were released by them based on the detailed engineering progressively. Therefore, OEM was fully dependent on JVP for the requirement of the parts specification so that subsequent activities of procurement could be undertaken. Further the import part was very critical, since these were to be procured under advance license (to avail the duty benefits of customs).

The procurement under advance license was a challenging, since there was no expertise available with OEM and responsibility rested on the procurement manager, who had very limited knowledge in this area. The domestic parts are those items which were to be procured in India; the procurement was to be undertaken post approval from the JVP so that the quality and the specifications are maintained. Most of the domestic items procured were of non-critical in nature and the same were utilised during fabrication and consumables that were required during the assembly of crane.

The quality department was responsible for the quality of the product at all stages from receipt of material to the dispatch of the crane. The whole organisation has evolved on quality-oriented culture due to the requirements of ISO and the API monogrammed facility. Hence the organisation processes were more skewed towards the quality. All the organisation and project process documentation (generation, circulation, storage, receipt, etc.) were also the additional responsibility of the quality department. The project documentation transmittal, a formal process for submission of project documentation to the customer, was also their responsibility.

Production was considered most important activity since the project deliverables were dependent upon the manufacturing, painting, and assembly with testing of the crane. The service department was responsible for assembly, however for the project execution restructuring of the organisation was carried out and the service department was brought under the production department on informal basis, this meant that service manager had to report to production head apart from COO and business development head for the service requirements. The service manager hence was put one level below in the organisation structure.

This project was accepted by OEM on the basis of commitment to adherence to the project agreed completion date. However prior to the contract acceptance, there were disagreements between OEM and JVP with respect schedule commitment. The project started based on the reservations by JVP of the project meeting the required performance criteria. The reason being additional crane project order was placed on the OEM by JVP and this was conflicting with the schedule (project in Case D). The design approval was also affected due to the classification agency included in the contract by end-user, since the vessel classed under the classification society of ABS. The project performance was affected by various reasons as follows: -

1. Engineering

    a. Non-availability of the design infrastructure

    b. Resource not adequate, for electrical, instrumentation and hydraulics

c. Delay in availability of design post detail engineering

d. Inter department conflicts due to project allocation to the engineering manager, hence conflict of interest between head of Department and his manager (since responsible for different projects)

e. Assembly drawings not available

2. Procurement

a. Late availability of Material Take Off (Raw material)

b. Material had to be procured as per the classification agency requirements

c. Only selected approved vendors by JVP

d. Terms of payments with vendors

e. Material had to be procured under advance license to avail the custom benefits

f. Too many agencies involved in the procurements

g. Domestic vendor not qualified

h. Non-payments to vendors

3. Production

a. Disorganised planning of the activities

b. Expertise not available since only one crane manufactured earlier

c. Conflict of interest in regard to

   i. Priority of fabrication

   ii. Responsibility of painting and assembly

    iii. Non-availability of material in domestic market

    iv. Adherence to JVP process

d. Liaising with external agencies

e. Vendor supports in-house

f. Non-availability of services in time

g. Incorrect status information to the stakeholders

h. Rework

i. Procurement or services taken during assembly at short notice

j. Workers safety, privilege, perks, etc.

k. Assembly expertise not available

4. Quality

    a. Supervision of the critical process

    b. Rework monitoring

    c. Communication with the external agencies and commitment

    d. By passing communication matrix

    e. Non -time bound activity, hence not integrated with the project schedule.

5. Project management

    a. Roles not defined properly

    b. Department not integrated with the processes

    c. Responsibility of the project, however no authority

    d. Multiple reporting

    e. No tracking of budget

    f. No resources in the department

    g. Scope not well-defined for tracking

    h. The project was handed over late and schedule did not have any control or check points

    i. Conflicts of production process with project management processes

6. Others

    a. No team building exercise for the team

    b. No motivational exercise

    c. Delayed payments to the staff

    d. Leaves not sanctioned for many

    e. No medical insurance

    f. Transport arrangements were under local vendors

    g. Logistic services were to be taken from the local vendors

    h. Issues related to the landowners and project affected families.

The procurements of bought-out parts were delayed in this project due to the non-availability of the specifications in time and ambiguity arising as, who to procure? since these items were supplied by JVP and in this project the order was directly on OEM.

During the execution, production activities at one point of time were ahead of schedule, but it got affected due to non-availability of few raw materials and bought out items required for manufacturing and assembly. The project often ran into many inter department issues pertaining to the ownership of the activities, "not my job" was very much existed in the organisation. Informal channels existed and informal power vested with few individuals, therefore the control of the project was difficult by COO and the project manager since course of the project depended upon few individual's inputs to the management rather than the domain heads.

The project suffered the cash flow requirements since the cash flow for the project was not taken into consideration. Due to this the payments to vendors/ sub vendors were affected, therefore after some time period lower channel partners refused to provide any assistance to OEM and stalled the supply of materials. This caused staggered material availability, and this affected the resource planning in production causing too many peaks and troughs relating to the resource usage and progress of work.

Contractor had been monitoring project based on the reports sent to them fortnightly, which was shown highly optimistic hence they were not able to understand the actual delay in the project. On verification of the project at facility, they realised that the project had got delayed beyond the buffer allocated for this project; hence customer stationed their expeditor at the facility. Based on the facts that Case progress was severely affected due to non-availability of the materials, contractor provided early payments to OEM to ensure that there is no further delay due to funds. The crane, one of the mandatory part for the platform for the roll out came became critical activity of the yard, since this had come into the critical path for the contractor in completion of the platform. In the final stage of assembly and testing, project faced few critical failures, and delay in availability of material further added to the delay of the project. During this stage the progress also got affected due to non-cooperation between few of the team members since there were abrupt changes in the production and assembly department. The team was stressed, as during the final stage of the project the teams had to work almost eighteen hours a day and sometime even full twenty four hours. This lead to high attrition in the organisation, one of the departments had an attrition rate of 100% and the organisation had attrition rate of 40%, which is considered as high in the industry.

Main contractor was cooperative despite the delay caused, they were interested in getting the work done in amicable way, during FAT all the minor issues and punch points were waived off and were undertaken by them at yard. The cranes delayed the platform project also. As soon as the cranes were received at yard, both the cranes were installed within twenty days from receipt at yard and the vessel sailed out the very next day to the completion of the SAT. The platform sailing was held up due to the crane projects incurring losses to the organisations.

On discussion with the project participants with regards to the macro factors, most of the project participants agreed that cost and scope were considered as the prime success criteria. The lack of cooperative and collaborative approach inter, and intra-organisation disallowed any positive interplay of intangible factors that were necessary for a project to be successful. The project activities such as planning, engineering procurement were being controlled by various five locations, which caused several communication related issues and was also one of the contributors towards the project delay. The external environment did not have any impact on the project performance, however in contrast internal environment had severe effect on the project results. Team members informed that there were no differentiations in approach towards managing the project and all projects were treated same. They carried out activities as directed by their supervisors or direct instructions from the top management. The individual performance were rated as per the departments, set goals which made the departments to compete with each other thereby creating non-cooperative approach. It was indicated that they preferred empowerment and decision-making authority at their level and domain. Therefore, they desired changes in the present organisation culture, which is employee friendly and integrated with other departments This could have enabled them to be more informed about the work being undertaken and align their efforts towards common goal.

Most of the project participants were demotivated due to various issues such as empowerment, respectability at work, working environment, compensation, unsafe environment, and job security. The team acknowledged the absence of the required intangible factors that were necessary to enhance the project performance. The nominated project manager lacked the requisite skills and experience that is necessary to execute any project. The motivation was low within the team members, and this was reflected in the form of attrition rate. Stakeholder analysis is critical and same was not undertaken by the OEM; in addition their project needs were not addressed appropriately.

The project was a failure from the iron triangle perspective, as it had exceeded the time and cost success criteria. In addition, from the stake holders, mainly end-user, project participants and other channel members this was termed as a failure project. The failure was attributed to absence of the right intangibles, due to which the objectives were not met and also the project participants were disappointed. The specification and WCA details of the case are provided in the final book.

Case D

The project in Case D was similar to the project as in Case C, as per the typology. All the variable attributes of the case remained same except one so that most appropriate results are achieved while mapping to the sensitivity analysis. The only variable deviant from Case C was the OEM, the project was awarded to the OEM JV partner instead of the OEM. The deliverables were similar to Case C, with all terms & condition also remaining the same. The platform with the cranes is shown at Figure 3.10.

Figure 3.10: Platform with Cranes

Introduction

JVP of the OEM was associated with the main contractor for several years as channel partner, the project was awarded to JVP with elements of trust and reliability. JVP had internally subcontracted the project to OEM. As a result, channel members and stakeholders involved in the project had increased as shown in Figure 3.11.

JVP provided support for engineering and project management activities of the Project. JVP was responsible for the contract since OEM being the subsidiary of the JVP. Main contractor was the purchaser of the product and responsible for the programme of the platform, roll out and handover to the owner's operation crew (team). The owner is the buyer of the platform, who would either be operating directly or through agencies for intended use of oil & gas exploration. The brief of the channel members is provided in subsequent subsections along with the project execution brief.

Channel Members

End-user

End-user remained the same as in the Case C, this was to understand the dynamics of project management of similar projects, analyse the results, and identify the factors responsible for the project outcome.

Main Contractor

The main contractor (contractor D) is a leading company focused on designing and executing complex offshore oil and gas projects worldwide. They are one of the largest US based engineering and construction companies exclusively focused on the upstream offshore oil and gas sector.

The company was incorporated in 1923, upon receipt of a contract to build fifty wooden drilling rigs, thereafter they have been expanding their business vigorously not only for new orders but also by acquiring various companies in the same field. Presently they are operating across the Atlantic, Middle East and Asia Pacific, and their integrated resources include approximately 13500 employees and a diversified fleet of marine vessel, fabrication facilities and engineering.

Main contractor has extensive experience of building oil and gas platforms, with a strong projectised matrix (PMPBOK, 2017) OS. The project was controlled by a project coordinator, who was at middle management level in the organisation, he was vested with authority to take decisions necessary for the project activities. The organisation had the concept of "cradle to Grave" approach, where the engineering team is responsible for all subproject of the platform till completion of the deliverables as per the contract.

OEM

Remained same as in Case C

Project Management Brief

JVP was associated with the contractor for several years as a global partner, hence the project was awarded to JVP for the elements of trust and reliability which was built over the years. JVP had internally subcontracted the project to OEM for the locational advantage, resulting in the increase of the channel members in the project as indicated in Figure 3.11.

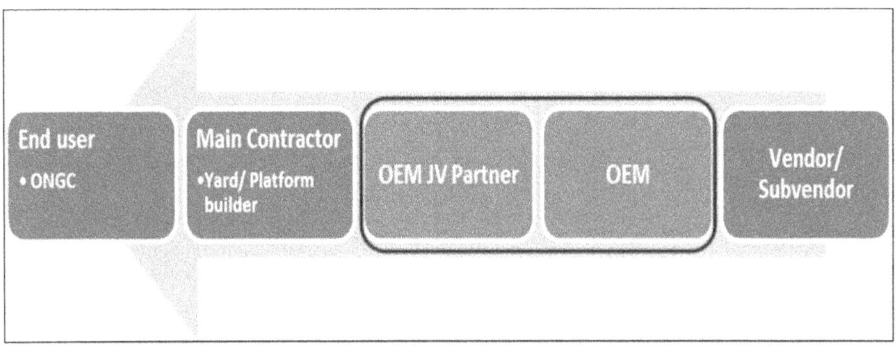

Figure 3.11: Case D - Channel partners

This project is perceived as successful by the project participants in contrast to Case C. The deliverables were similar to Case C, with identical scope and type of contract, only difference in the scope was the number of cranes, total of four cranes were to be delivered against instead of the two cranes as in the case C. The project details of the case are as indicated in Table 3.7.

Table 3.7: Case D - Project details

S.No	Criteria	Data/Information	Remarks
1	Scope	Design, manufacture, supply, and commissioning of API monogrammed Crane	Fixed
2	Cost	19 Crores (04 cranes)	Fixed
3	Time (project duration)	10, 10.5, 11 and 11.5 months respectively	Fixed duration, except for erection and SAT
4	Contract type	EPM – Engineering Procurement, management (Installation & commissioning supervision)	Turnkey type – Cost of management additional

S.No	Criteria	Data/Information	Remarks
5	Organisations structure (OS)	Modified - strong matrix (Kerzner, 2013, PMBOK, 2008)	OS provided authority to the project manager with appropriate reporting structure. Key factor for the project success.
6	Immediate customer	JV Partner	JVP were directly handling main contractor
7	Channel members	Five (including OEM)	The order was on the JV partner, hence extra channel level

In the initial phase of the project execution, less cooperation existed inter and intra-organisation. Due to additional channel member within the OEM organisation caused the establishment of informal organisations structure in the OEM organisation which created confusion among the team members. This was due to dual reporting for the team members as well as sudden culture shift which needed to be aligned to the requirements of the JVP standards. Therefore, on realising the confusions within the team, JVP redefined the roles & responsibilities, replaced the project manager and the expectations by the members towards the project. By restructuring of project OS and by introduction of communication matrix with all stakeholders, there was continuous improvement in the cooperation as the project progressed. The reorganised OS, project management and decision-making dynamics are as shown in Figure 3.12.

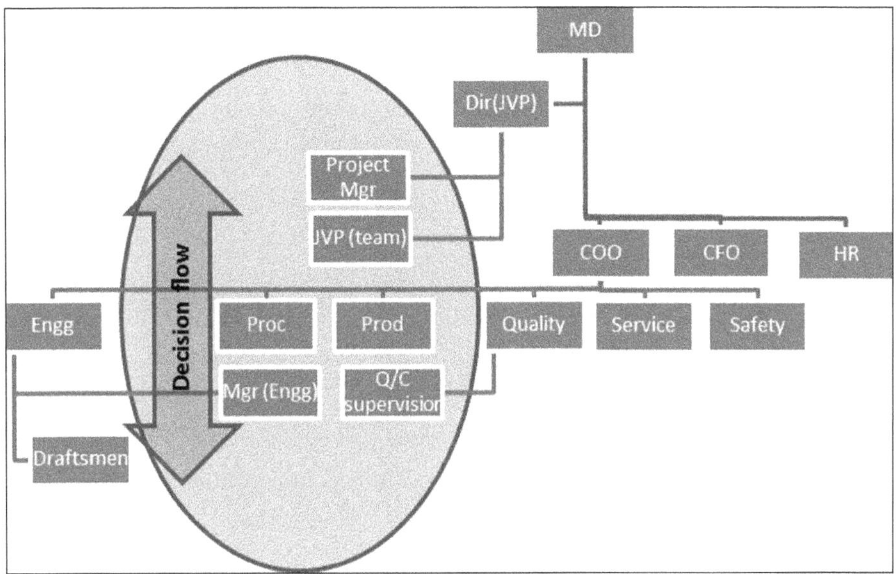

Figure 3.12: Case D - Project organisation and management

The schedule was defined as one of the main project objectives, despite multiple projects being executed simultaneously within the OEM organisation, where there were clashes of the delivery dates. The resources were optimised by hiring additional manpower as required for multiple projects. The projects were reprioritised to have minimal deviations against their deliveries to all the projects. The trust factor, inter and intra-organisation started improving as the project progressed. The motivation level of the JVP and OEM teams also improved. This was due to introduction and adaptation of collaborative & participative decision-making approach. The team was more focused and cohesive in this case, and this was due to the leadership and good communication skills of the project manager. JVP adapted a methodical process-oriented approach, ensuring that the project was being executed as a process, thus ascertaining that all team members contributed towards achieving project objectives.

Import purchases for the project were managed directly by JVP, and the procurement processes were not impacted due to the business relationship built over the years. However, erratic domestic supplies affected the project, as domestic vendors stalled the supplies for non-receipt of payments in time by the OEM. JVP, therefore released additional interim funds on an immediate basis to ensure the supplies enabled them to get the schedule under control. However, similar to Case C, the delivery of the last two cranes was delayed by twenty days due to the inauguration ceremony of the new facility.

Despite arduous efforts by the project team, the project deviated slightly as per the success criteria. The project was considered successful by the team and stakeholders, since the delay was curtailed drastically, and the platform schedule was unaffected. End-user and main contractor appreciated the JVP's efforts in expending resources at high cost for the cause of the project thereby enabling them to launch the platform as per schedule. The PM details are as provided in Table 3.8.

Table 3.8: Case D - Project management details

S.No	Criteria	Data/Information	Remarks
1	Project manager skills	Experienced and skilled	Project decision-making was vested with project manager. On change of OS, & project manager the performance of the project was improved

S.No	Criteria	Data/Information	Remarks
2	Communication	Adequate as per kick off formal & informal	Communication internal and external helped is fast resolution of issues and project performance
3	Channel partners Relationship	Good - except with OEM & domestic vendors	Most of the channel members were channel partners for long time. However, relationship with OEM and domestic vendors were strained
4	Stakeholders - management	Stake holder analysis not undertaken. However, managed appropriately	As new entrant into the Indian industry stake holder analysis is critical. OEM did not carry out the analysis; however, JVP managed the stakeholder's appropriately with focus on schedule and customer satisfaction.
5	Decision-Making	Project manager	Informed decisions were taken, with responsibility of the project manager.

Project Execution

The project negotiation for this contract was held between the main contractor and JVP. The negotiation of the project was smooth since JVP were known to the main contractor hence the project contract was finalised and accepted with technical and brief commercial discussions.

The project was awarded to JVP due to the reputation in the industry and good relationship with the contractor, which was built over the years, hence commitment towards adherence to the quality and agreed schedule was well understood as deliverables. Post receipt of the Project, the project was subcontracted to the OEM (excluding the engineering) since the customer & end-user were from India, this made JVP as the immediate customer of OEM within their organisation. The main contractor had nominated an experienced project coordinator to oversee the project. The coordinator was at middle level in the OS and was empowered to take decisions with regards to the project, as he had the expertise of the crane and projects. The main contractor had the concept of "Cradle to Grave" where in the team involved during the design stage would oversee full project till commissioning of the project. The communications process was well-defined, with the coordinator being the one point of contact for all activities. The defined process intended that all the issues were communicated to coordinator, who would resolve the matter in his capacity or coordinate with his team and ensure the same is communicated to JVP project manager.

The project performance with regards to the schedule had deviated considerably affecting all stakeholders, therefore JVP restructured the OS to a strong project matrix. A dedicated project manager was nominated and supported by project coordinator (engineering manager) from the OEM organisation.

In this case, the initiation of the project was undertaken by handing over the project formally to the project manager in an internal kick off meeting along with internal contract review and handing over of internal work order. The internal work order is a document which defines the project scope in detail, so that whenever internal participants have any ambiguity, they can refer to this document for clarity. The project schedule was prepared based on the PO with fixed dates, the micro level schedule was prepared in MSP tool. The project manager was well versed with the tool, hence the deviations were tracked and controlled by the tool as necessary. The project manager also tracked the milestone-based performance criteria and was empowered to take decisions accordingly. The role and responsibilities for project manager and team members were well-defined with proper reporting structure. The decision-making was decentralised, and project team members were also empowered to take decisions as necessary for the project.

The engineering phase was as per the schedule as the approval processes were curtailed at JVP. OEM received all the approved drawings during the production phase of the project. The OEM procurement department had very limited role since most activities were carried out by JVP, procurement department was responsible for the domestic procurement, import/ export, excise, receipt of all material and dispatch of the entire crane in knock down condition (disassembled state). The participants involved in the procurement process were OEM procurement, quality and JVP procurement, quality & project departments respectively.

In this case, responsibility for ensuring the project was executed and completed in all aspects vested with JVP. However, one of the high-risk zone and critical activity was import procurements since these were to be procured under advance license (to avail the duty benefits of customs). This was a challenging process, since there was no expertise available with OEM and the responsibility rested with the procurement manager, who had very limited knowledge in this domain. The domestic procurements (items to be procured in India) list was provided with necessary specifications by the JVP, thus ensuring that items are procured as per the requisite specifications. Most of the domestic items were non-critical in nature and the same were utilised during fabrication and consumables that were required during the assembly of crane.

The quality department was responsible for the quality of the product at all stages from receipt of material to the dispatch of the crane. The JVP organisation had evolved on the quality-oriented culture due to the requirements of ISO and the API monogrammed facility requirements. Hence the organisation processes were more skewed towards the quality. The project process documentation was very important, and responsibility was placed with the quality department. This being a critical process, the project documentation transmittals, formal process for submission of project documentation to the customer was undertaken by the JVP itself.

Production is the most critical and important activity, since the project deliverables were dependent upon the manufacturing, painting, assembly and testing of the crane. Prior to restructuring of the OS, the project was delayed due to low prioritisation of the projects by OEM. Therefore, during reorganisation JVP placed their supervisor to ensure that the production and assembly activities are controlled appropriately to improve the schedule performance. The project confronted many challenges, and the project performances were impacted severely before restructuring, however these were curtailed post restructuring, and the schedule performance were improved even by expending additional cost than the assigned budget.

The various reasons that influenced the project prior to restructuring and post restructuring of OS are as mentioned below:-

1. Engineering

    a. Inter department conflicts due to project allocation to the engineering manager as assistant project coordinator, hence conflict of interest between head of Department (project manager for Case C project)

    b. Assembly drawings not available

2. Procurement

    a. Material had to be procured under advance license to avail the custom benefits

    b. Domestic vendors not qualified

    c. Non-payments to vendors, who had stalled the supplies

3. Production

    a. Disorganised way of planning the activities

    b. Expertise not available since only one crane manufactured earlier

    c. Conflict of interest in

        i. Priority of fabrication

        ii. Responsibility of painting and assembly

      iii. Non- availability of material

      iv. Adherence to JVP processes

      v. Non- availability of services in time

      vi. Rework

      vii. Procurement or services required during assembly at short notice

      viii. Worker's safety, privilege, perks, etc.

4. Quality

    a. Supervision of the critical process

    b. Rework monitoring

    c. Non- time bound activity, hence, not integrated with project schedule.

5. Project management

    a. Department not integrated with the processes

    b. Multiple reporting for project coordinator

    c. OEM production process contradiction with project management processes

6. Others

    a. No team building exercise for the team

    b. Delayed payments to the staff

    c. Leaves not being sanctioned for the work force

    d. No medical insurance

    e. Transport arrangements were under local vendors

    f.   Logistic services were to be taken from the local vendors

    g.   Issues related to the landowners and project affected families.

The production of the major assemblies at one point of time was behind the planned schedule by approximately two and half months, however this was expedited by reallocation of the resources and converging to this specific project. Contractor had been monitoring the project very closely and the reports submitted were most realistic, hence on understanding that the project was out of track, an expeditor was placed at OEM facility. This was to ensure that all issues are resolved instantly by participative method at the facility itself. The project was not affected by other various inter department conflicts with respect to ownership of the activities. The reason being project manager ensured that there was little interference from OEM higher management in decision-making unless escalated as per the process.

The project initially got afflicted by negative cash flow, nevertheless same was attended on priority and funds were released by JVP as necessary despite deviating from agreed upon milestone payments. The initial funds released for the project were diverted for purpose other than projects thus affecting the payments to lower channel members.

In the final stage of assembly and testing, the project encountered few import procurements related issues, the same were resolved immediately due to JVP better liaising with the suppliers (foreign vendors). In addition, in the last stage of project, few of the team members did not cooperate due to abrupt changes in the production and assembly departments, the issues were brought under control by ensuring that the directives of the project manager and the JVP supervisors will be upheld. The team members in this project were motivated and less stressed due to the sub-work culture (to OEM organisation culture) that existed in this Project. Therefore, the delay of three months could be improved by one month and the delay curtailed to two months. The improvement in the schedule helped in ensuring that the platform schedule was not affected. Due to the phenomenal efforts and cost expended by JVP, main contractor and end-user were contented and appreciative, therefore despite schedule delay there was no LD levied.

Most of the project participant participants confirmed that consideration of end-user satisfaction and project objectives were the catalyst for better project performance. The schedule and quality were considered as the prime success criteria to meet the end-user and main contractor project objectives. The cooperative and collaborative approaches, inter and intra-organisation post restructuring of the OS enabled positive interplay of tangible and intangible factors, which was vital for the project to be successful. The external environment did not have any impact on the project performance, but the internal environment, as stated was vital, this earlier had negative and later constructive effect on the project results in terms of cooperative and collaborative approach. Team members informed that there were no differentiations in approach towards managing the project, all projects were treated same in the early stages later the same was changed. However, post restructuring, team members were empowered to take decisions in the interest of the project requirements. This helped the team members in converging their efforts towards common the project objectives. The team acknowledged the presence of positive intangible factors, which enhanced the project performance. The project manager played a critical role in the integration of the organisation and key stakeholders.

The project deviated slightly from the iron triangle perspective, as the cost and schedule, success criteria were not met. Nonetheless, as the severe deviations were curtained, and no stakeholder was affected the project was termed as successful. The project participants and the key stakeholders were appreciative with regards to the resources applied and efforts put in to improve the project schedule. The perceived project success was attributed to the presence of the right intangible factors, due to which the objective could be met. The cost of the project had increased, due to which the project margins were reduced (yet positive). In addition, the main contractor did not levy LD on the JVP thereby contributing towards cost project success criterion positively. The specification and WCA details of the case are provided in the final book.

Case E

Introduction

The final case study is a retrofit (removal and re-fitment) type of project from oil and gas sector with a different set of deliverable and higher complexity. The project considered is EPIM type of contract, which includes re-engineering, procurement, manufacturing, installation management and conducting the sea acceptance trials (SAT).

Figure 3.13: Offshore Support vessel

The retrofit project involved renewal of remote-controlled propulsion system including replacement of various other associated equipments of offshore support vessel as shown in the Figure 3.13 for reference. The systems included hydraulic, electrical, electronic, and mechanical systems (excluding thrusters). This project was comparatively complex compared to other projects as mentioned earlier, one of the main reasons being multiple internal stakeholders, agencies and critical interrelated time bond activities involved in the execution of project.

The project selected in this case is from the oil and gas sector in marine industry. The project is executed on multipurpose offshore vessel, which is into service of oil exploration. Vessel is owned by OIL and Natural Gas Corporation (ONGC), however operations, manning, maintenance, operation and management (O&M) services is by Shipping Corporation of India (SCI) for ONGC. The selected project is of a retrofit type, renewal of remote-controlled propulsion system which included replacement of various equipments of the system; the hydraulic, electric electronic and mechanical system excluding thrusters. The thrusters of the vessels were to be overhauled completely with replacement of critical functional part and if any damaged parts are found during the disassembly such that the equipment is functional for the remaining life cycle of the vessel. Out of four thrusters, two were 100% operational, one could be operated only to its 60% efficiency, and one could not be used due to excessive vibration. The major deliverables are supply of all propulsion equipments along with the system, in addition it had dual classification - DNV and IRS. The project included re-engineering, procurement, supply, FAT, erection, commissioning, and SAT. The contract is EPIM type, where engineering content involved is re-engineering of old system up-gradation to new system with full functionality and modifications to earlier design, manufacturing and supply of all critical equipments including pipes cabling, connecting up at various compartment and supervision of activities involved with other agencies. The total project schedule is twelve months, however, was dependent upon the availability of the dry-dock slot with the yard/ main contractor. This project is awarded by the OEM Wartsila (Netherland), however the project was jointly undertaken by Wartsila Netherland and India due to the global process set-up. The channel partners involved in the case are as shown at Figure 3.14.

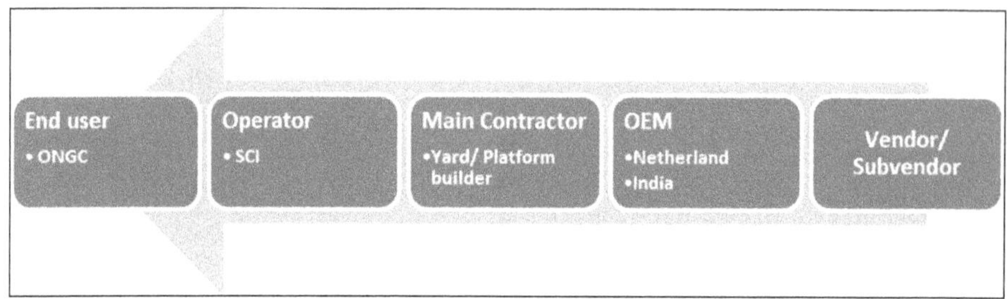

Figure 3.14: Case E - Channel partners

The role of all channel members remained the same, however in this case there was an additional channel member "Operator". This channel member is vessel operator who accepted the O&M contract of the vessel. Under O&M contract they are responsible for the operation and necessary maintenance of the vessel so that the business objective of their organisation and the end-user for the oil & gas exploration activities are delivered. They are responsible for the vessel brown field projects, who are responsible for ensuring the deliverables are defined and met for the intended use. The brief of the channel members are provided in the subsequent section.

Channel Members

The project channel member in this case consisted of end-user (ONGC), Operator (SCI), main contractor (yard) -Cochin shipyard Limited (CSL), OEM Wartsila India, vendors/ suppliers / service provider for raw material and readily available off the shelf parts/ equipment.

End-User

End-user remained the same as in the case of C & D.

Operator

Shipping Corporation of India (SCI) is a Government of India Public Sector Enterprise with its headquarters in Mumbai that operates and manages vessels that services both national and international lines. SCI was established on 2nd October 1961 by the amalgamation of Eastern Shipping Corporation and Western Shipping Corporation. Two more shipping companies, Jayanti Shipping Company and Mogul Lines Limited, were merged with SCI in 1973 and 1986 respectively. SCI started out with ninteen vessels. It gradually metamorphosed into a conglomerate having eighty ships with interests in different segments of the shipping trade. It also manages thirty nine vessels on behalf of various government departments and other organisations. The services provided are, Liner and passenger services, Bulk carrier and tanker services, offshore services and Liquefied Natural Gas. Major clients being, Indian Oil Corporation Ltd, Bharat Heavy Electricals Ltd, Steel Authority of India Ltd, Oil and Natural Gas Corporation Ltd, Reliance Industries Ltd, Bharat Petroleum Corporation Limited, Hindustan Petroleum Corporation Ltd, British Petroleum, British Gas, Shell, and Tata. SCI was also awarded the prestigious 'Navratna' status by Indian Government in 2008.

The offshore services department provides vessel services such as, Towing and Anchor handling operations in Offshore, carry out standby and rescue operations in offshore, if required. Carry out routine surveillance offshore for safety and security reasons,

Standby at SBM Tankers Offshore and Carry out Fire Fighting duties by FIFI vessels. SCI also offers Operations, manning, maintenance, and management (O&M) services of following vessels owned by Indian Exploration and Production (E&M) Company, Oil and Natural Gas Corporation Ltd. (ONGC):

Main Contractor (EPCM/ Yard)

Cochin Shipyard Ltd (CSL) is the largest green field ship building and ship repair yard in the country, situated adjacent to the port of Cochin in the west coast of India. The yard is built on 170 acres of land, out of which sixty acres is set aside for future expansion. Cochin Shipyard was incorporated in the year 1972 as a fully owned Government of India company. The yard commenced the shipbuilding operations in 1978, ship repair in 1981, Marine Engineering Training in 1993 and Offshore Up-gradation in 1999.

In the last three decades the company has emerged as a forerunner in the Indian Shipbuilding and Ship repair industry. This yard can build and repair the largest vessels in India. It can build ships up to 1,10,000 DWT and repair ships up to 1,25,000 DWT. The yard has delivered two of India's largest double hull Aframax tankers each of 95,000 DWT. CSL is also building the country's first indigenous Air Defence Ship which was launched very recently. Only Shipyard in India which can repair, Air Defence Ship, undertake complex and sophisticated repairs to Oil Rigs; and ships of Navy, Coast Guard and Merchant Navy, major projects from ONGC for repairs of Mobile Offshore Drilling Unit (MODU) and Jack Up Rig (JUR).

OEM -

End-user remained the same as in the Case A & B.

Project Management Details

This project also involved a high dependence on several external factors for successful completion. The project details are provided in Table 3.9.

The initiation of the project was undertaken after adequate due diligence and a well-defined scope arrived at with participation of required channel members. The technical negotiation was also undertaken using a participative method to ensure clarity in the scope and integration of roles and responsibilities.

The schedule was made flexible depending upon two major external dependent factors, namely, availability of ship and dry-dock. OEM followed the proper project processes and ensured that all the dimensions of the defined scope were verified for proper understanding with the channel partners in the external kick off meeting. The initial phase of the project was delayed as per the risks anticipated in the risk register ("Known- Unknown," PMBOK 2008). However, the same was mitigated innovatively as per a prepared response plan. This was possible as top managements in end-user, operator, main contractor, and OEM were flexible and open to new ideas and its execution as necessary. Stakeholder analysis was undertaken by the OEM so that their concerns were addressed by proper communication and attending to the expressed needs or requirements. Lot of preparatory work was carried out to ensure that there was no delay in timely availability of resources.

Table 3.9: Case E - Project details

S.No	Criteria	Data/Information	Remarks
1	Scope	Retrofit of Propulsion system with supply of new equipment and SAT.	Flexible - Up-gradation of remote-control propulsion system excluding the engines.
2	Cost	₹ 14.28 Crores	Fixed for the identified and flexible for scope and schedule change was anticipated
3	Time (project duration)	Nine months	For the defined scope, excluding SAT
4	Contract type	EPM - Engineering, Procurement, management (Installation & commissioning supervision)	Modified Turnkey type
5	Organisation structure (OS)	Modified strong matrix (Kerzner, 2013, PMBOK, 2008)	The project managers had the control over all project activities.
6	Immediate customer	O&M contractor (SCI)	The order was executed by two companies of Wartsila - Netherland & India
7	Channel members	Five	OEM considered one channel member since working together, though the order was split intra-company

The initial phases of the project witnessed many intra-organisational conflicts as several OEM, contractor and sub-contractors were attending the vessel project. This was resolved in a participative matter. Main contractor and operator took joint responsibility for allocating critical resource so that any delay would not be attributable to them. The notable observation is that OEM and main contractor project manager jointly planned the activities so as to integrate them with other stakeholders attending the vessel activities. The OEM had a unique hybrid strong matrix type OS as shown in the Figure 3.15, in which the project management activities were undertaken.

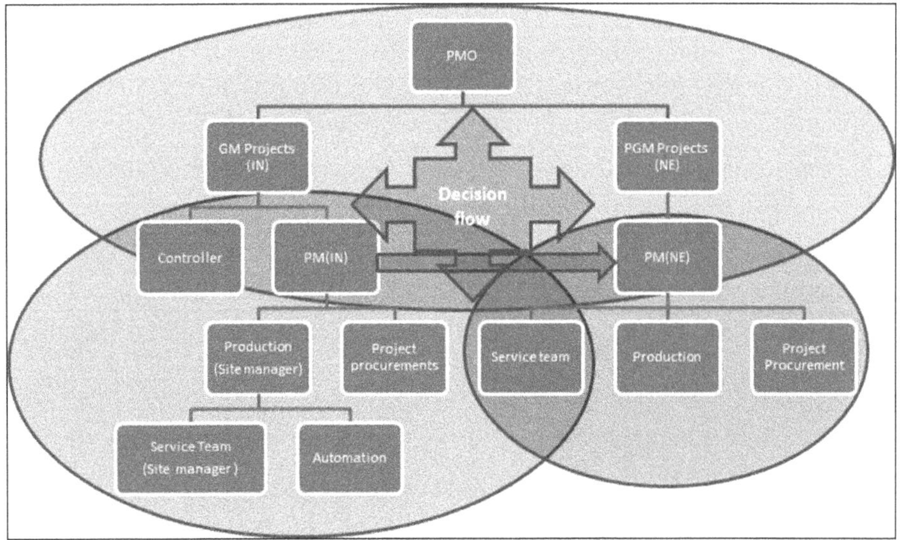

Figure 3.15: Case E - Project organisation and management

Project managers were fully empowered and responsible for the project decisions. The team was also empowered to take decisions in their individual capacities. Project participants ensured that there was no delay in the project due to pending decisions.

The roles and responsibilities were well-defined and documented into the necessary matrix. There did exist intra-organisation conflicts, however they were resolved at the appropriate levels without hampering the project schedule. Further, co-location of project participants during the peak of the project implementation enhanced the project performance. Co-location of the team helped not only in better participative decision-making, but also in building trust within the project participants necessary for such a collaborative approach. Informal meetings inter and intra-organisation helped in resolving major issues which were later documented and accepted formally by the requisite project participants.

The project objective was well-defined and in line with the organisational goals, thus helping project participants to converge their efforts towards the same goal. The major objective was to ensure that the schedule incorporates the requirements of all major stakeholders. The scope and cost of the project was kept flexible from the beginning as the team in view of the anticipated changes to the external factors and "known unknown" risks. The project witnessed notable scope change, extension in duration thus increase in cost as well. Though the success criteria pertaining to scope, time and cost underwent variations, the project was still considered a success. The project was a success as per the iron triangle also since the original scope was met in time and cost. The project had achieved higher perceived success as it met the objectives of most of the channel partners and satisfied the end customer. The project management details are as provided in Table 3.10.

Table 3.10: Case E - Project management details

S.No	Criteria	Data/ Information	Remarks
1	Project manager skills	PMP and experienced	Both project managers were at mid-level in the organisation
2	Communication	Adequate as per the kick off formal & informal	Communication internal and external, helped in fast resolution of issues and project performance
3	Channel partners Relationship	Initially conflicts inter organisation, however, was improved to greater extent on subsequent stages	Positive relationship. Worked as a team, not only across cross channel partners but also with other OEM and contractors working onboard vessel external to channel chain.
4	Stakeholders - management	Yes – by OEM	The stakeholder analysis was undertaken by OEM to ensure all the stake holders' needs are taken care towards the committed scheduled date as high priority.
5	Decision-Making	Decentralised - Towards customer requirements of operation ability - objectives	The decision-making was well-defined for the team for both inter and intra-organisation companies
6	Cultural issues	Initially yes	Existed, addressed by co-location and team building.

Project Execution

The project was awarded to Wartsila Netherland (OEM) due to the OEM global structure. However the project was executed by Wartsila Netherland and India together. The project was executed in India at main contractor (yard) Cochin Shipyard Ltd, Cochin.

The vessel operator had accepted the contract of manning, operation, and maintenance of the vessel on behalf of the end-user. The vessel was due for it major maintenance, therefore the contract for dry-docking and maintenance activities of the vessel was awarded to CSL. All the maintenance related activities were part of their yard scope; however OEM related activities were to be undertaken by the OEM or prequalified vendor for those equipments by ONGC. In this case of negotiation was in two phases, technical and commercial. Since the total vessel maintenance contract was awarded to CSL, the operator included CSL is the technical negotiation for this project, as the scope of OEM and yard were interlinked. To ensure that the battery limits of the project interface are well understood and accepted, it was agreed by both the OEM and yard to be part of the negotiation. The technical and scope negotiation took place between operator (ship superintendent, technical and procurement rep), yard and the OEM. The negotiations underwent three iterations, to ensure that the RFP is well understood, and the scope is optimal enough so that the vessel is able to operate for the rest of its life cycle.

The negotiation was based the on the proposed plan and duration of the project, since vessel operations was of high priority and critical due to oil exploration activities, hence the essence of time was very critical with flexibility of schedule period and not the duration (duration was kept fixed since availability and the docking of vessel dates could vary). Tentative schedule plans were prepared as per the forecast availability of the vessel and dry-dock. Both event happenings were challenges due to the critical operations being handled by them and high uncertainty of availability. Therefore ensuring all dry-docking activities during the dry-dock period was very important by all channel members for the project to be successful. The macro plan was prepared and circulated so that the interfacing activities are integrated as common plan without hampering any other projects being undertaken on the same vessel.

The commercial negotiation was held only between the operator and the OEM. The costing was provided to the operator with broad breakup of equipments and resource cost. A further list of all imported parts was listed separately for the duty exemption certificate for these equipments could be availed.

The project started with issuance of the project charter by nominating the project manager and authorising him to expend resources for the project. Internal project kickoff meeting was conducted by the sales the team to hand over the project, to project manager and the team with all key information and creating the project in the ERP and gateway system. After necessary internal process and procedures external kick off was held with the operator SCI and main contractor (yard). In the external kick off the scope, schedule and the integration interface were reconfirmed with all project participants. The internal kick off also initiated other activities in parallel such as re-engineering, procurement.

The OEM project OS consisted of project manager (Netherland), project manager (India), site manager, team leads and site teams as core team and other department managers such as account, business control, procurement etc. project also saw inter organisation conflicts since two sister companies (India and Netherland) were involved in the project, and six teams from various departments were directly involved in the project execution. The issues such as decision-making, roles and responsibilities, inter department goals, cultural, division of the contract, etc., and these issues were attended by various means such as, converging the project objectives and goal, linking issues with individual/ department / organisation performance bonus, replacement of individuals, visits by department heads to site, daily meeting by project manager with site teams and other department directly involved in the project execution activities, etc.

The project was divided into two subprojects viz import and domestic related activities. Import activities included manufacturing of the OEM equipments and procurement of imported items required for the project. The domestic related activities included site activities on vessels availability, procurement of domestic items required during retrofit, overhaul of thrusters. A micro plan of these activities was prepared by the respective nominated leads and same was integrated with the macro plan. A top to bottom planning approach was carried out since the durations were fixed, however with tentative dates.

During early phase of project one of the major risks triggered of non-availability of the vessel in time, due to which the other activities durations became critical, therefore major activities which were to be undertaken at OEM site and during dry-docking had become critical. OEM proposed an innovative approach of hiring a temporary facility for two months near the yard so that time taken for transportation of the thrusters to and from could be avoided (approximately four weeks). A workshop was taken on lease for two months and the same was modified so that all activities with respect to overhaul and FAT could be undertaken. Since the vessel was not available in time the next slot of docking was scheduled, the docking was also in two phases to ensure the optimal utilisation of the dock. In the first phase, the underwater equipments were removed, and external opening were blanked so that the vessel could float and taken out of the dock. On completion of the routines on the onboard equipments, the vessel was re-docked for the re-fitment of and other various activities necessary to be completed prior to undocking.

Various teams, such as site management, retrofit team, service team, sub-contractors, overhaul, etc... who were to be mobilised were on standby at their respective facilities and were being utilised for other project activities and could be mobilised at one day notice for the optimal utilization. On confirmation of the vessel availability, one team was boarded on the vessel for pre-check and pre-work activities which was scheduled to be undertaken post arrival of vessel at yard. These activities were undertaken while the vessel sailed from Mumbai to Cochin. All the teams were made available in three days, prior to the arrival of the vessel, at CSL yard with completion of the necessary administrative requirements. The planning was done in minute details of time management such as stay, food, transportation, etc., to ensure that minimum or no time is lost.

On arrival of the vessel, few of the activities were executed ahead of the scheduled plan, therefore subsequent activities were re-planned as per the fronts available in the vessel, and the same was continued on daily basis. On the commencement of the project, within a few days conflicts started with the various sub-contractors, yard and the OEM's working in the same area. Therefore, immediately a meeting was called and as per the priorities the compartments were divided into zones and the clearances were provided accordingly. This helped in ensuring that the activities are synchronised as per the priorities with holistic view and ensuring that no activities is lagging or leading and creating holding times in the schedule.

Vessel docking was further delayed due to urgent requirement of Naval ship docking, defence related activities always supersed the docking schedule for the operational requirements. This unanticipated risk led to further compression of the vessel docking schedule. Therefore to overcome this delay, a simulated set-up was made, such that templates, fixtures, and planning of activities in detail were undertaken. The teams involved were more than fifteen while docking and four teams required for the project activities of first phase of docking, the excise mentioned helped the team to remove all the thruster in a short period and ensured the hull bottom were blanked for vessel to float. The vessel was then floated so that the next phase of the activities could be undertaken afloat.

During the afloat of the vessel (post first undocking), various activities of removal and installation of equipments were undertaken. There were a few activities which were to be carried out by the yard and were interconnected with various OEM's or sub-contractors working on board. These services became constrained due to multiple requirements at multiple places at one instant. This further led to conflicts between the multiple subcontractors and OEM's working, since the service was to be provided by yard and were also responsible for the vessel project. To resolve the conflicts, the scope and the time schedule was revisited, and the service priorities were defined to ensure that the activities are sequenced as per the fronts available, and the services are provided accordingly. The yard also instructed sub-contractors to increase the teams required for such services so that there were adequate teams available to attend the activities to avoid delays. Such type of intra-organisation conflicts was resolved in daily morning meetings chaired by the project manager of the main contractor and attended by all project manager or the appointed coordinators of all organisations at site. If any issues which could not be resolved would be escalated with their respective higher authorities, however till the time the issue is resolved the earlier decision taken in the meeting will be advocated.

During the next phase of docking, the activities were progressing well, when unanticipated risk triggered, during the dry trials of the equipments. One of the thrusters which were earlier used only in emergency, experienced excessive vibrations and was not completely lowering to the required depth. On re-examining the defect, it was found that there was deflection in the hull due to hot work carried out in the past. Rectification of this work required an additional eleven days of docking since thruster were to be removed again for the rectification and the re-trial (FAT) to be undertaken prior to dispatch. Neither the yard nor the client could schedule this activity, therefore the decision was taken that the vessel would sail with only three functional thrusters, and whenever the vessel would be available for the repairs, the activity would be undertaken. Therefore the all the trials were completed successfully with three thrusters and the vessel sailed for its required commitment.

To make the fourth thruster operational, docking was scheduled after three months based on the availability of vessel and dry-dock at yard. This docking was undertaken for a very short period of eleven days and all the required activities for hull repairs and making thruster operation was undertaken. This time there were no notable conflicts since this was the only activity to be undertaken during the dry-dock. The other minor activities and punch points were being undertaken onboard the vessel. This activity was carried out on approval of the scope change request by the respective authorities, as no Control Change Board was defined.

Discussion with the project participants with regards to the macro factors confirmed that end-user satisfaction and project objectives were considered as key to positive project results. The schedule and quality were considered as the prime success criteria along with the end-user and operator operational requirements as project objectives, which influenced the project to success. The cooperative and collaborative approaches, inter and intra-organisation enabled positive interplay of tangible and intangible factors which played vital role in the project to be successful. The external environment, of non-availability of vessel did delay the project, however due to positive interplay of the intangibles in the internal environment provided innovative ways for a project to be successful. The team members were empowered to take decisions in the interest of the project and organisation. This helped the team members to converge their efforts towards common project objectives. OEM in this case mentioned that the projects were classified based on the risk as Class A, B or C and the approach towards different class project was different. This classification helped the organisation to optimise the resources and priorities the projects in the portfolio with requisite attention of the management.

The team acknowledged the presence of intangible factors which enhanced the project performance. The project managers played a vital role in inter and intra-organisation integration and decision-making in the uncertain environment. OEM had undertaken the stakeholder analysis, so that their needs are well understood from project perspective and are attended appropriately.

The project was a successful project from the iron triangle perspective, as the time, cost and quality success criteria were achieved. The project achieved the required objectives despite being confronted with several constraints, therefore the stakeholders, end-user, project participants and other channel members perceived the project as successful. The success of the project was attributed to the presence of the right intangibles, due to which the objectives could be met, and this also influenced the tangible success criteria.

The performance of the project was much above the specified performance parameters with regards to the iron triangle as well as the intangible factors. The WCA of the case is provided in the final book.

Summary

The aim of this book was mainly to provide the project practitioners and students exposure to the micro level project dynamics through the case studies, thus enabling them to improve the project performance. The objective of complete study is to explore and identify the factors responsible for marine project success in India and examine the adequacy of the currently accepted criteria for measuring the performance and success of a project. This was Stage Two and part of the complete study as indicated of descriptive type. The second stage comprised of multiple case studies to facilitate an in-depth understanding of the PM and validation of the identified factors.

This stage of study comprised an in-depth study of polar marine projects that offered literal as well as theoretical replication, which would help the readers to understand and analyse the dynamics of the project. Reading the final book shall enable the readers to undertake the WCA & CCA. The approach established that there does exist a correlation between the two categories which is also known as interplay. The approach adopted by the organisation towards project management with regard to the success criteria does impact the project success or failure. The cases do indicate that human-related factors are vital in the project environment, and they are also critical to the project as well as the organisation. The cases also established the validity of the SFs identified from the first stage of the study, and also negated the success criteria with regards to the iron triangle.

In the CCA, all the fourteen SFs were comparatively evaluated across the five cases depending on the project management approach adopted with respect to the success criteria, the interplay of tangible and intangible factors and their effect on project success or failure. Results of cross case analysis were in contrast to the polar cases mainly due to the approach of the success criteria and effects of the intangibles. The cross-case analysis also highlighted that all the members of the project channel are critical for the project success, and they need to be integrated with respect to the common objective of the end-user requirements.

Scope for Future Study

As mentioned earlier, less study has been undertaken in the marine sector globally in regard to project success or failure with holistic approach. This study has the limitation in regard to the Indian context and the type of the projects selected for the case study. Therefore, study can be extended to global context with comparison of the PM approach by the various countries. Further there is scope for narrowing the research to shipbuilding and oil and gas sector and if necessary for government and private organisation. Further, quantitative analysis of the identified success criteria and success factors with correlation between them can be checked to generalise the findings.

Sample Quotes From Project Practitioners

Sample quotes from project practitioners indicating factor responsible for the project performance

Sample Quotes	Factor
The project performance is drastically affected if the **status reporting** is not appropriate, the facts related to schedule delay is not reported or mitigation plans are not achievable.	Communication
Project cannot exist without **communication.**	Communication
The project participants and stakeholder need to be **appropriately communicated** with the required information, for timely decisions thereby controlling the project performance.	Communication
95% of the project manager role involves communication with stake holders or activities for communication such as **reports, pre and post meeting activities**, preparation of issue resolutions.	Communication
With proper **communication** in regard to the project scope and objectives, we can take proactive measure which will help the project performance.	Communication
Profit making is the key to the business objective of every project hence cannot be isolated.	Cost
The **cost** is the key driver for the other factors of scope, schedule, and the quality, hence cannot be ignored at all.	Cost

Sample Quotes	Factor
Projects will not exist without **cost,** even if they **make losses** as the portfolio and programme should be positive margin and in line with the organisation's goals.	Cost
The lower channel members were more interested in **maximising** their own **profits** by focusing only on the cost rather than the objective of the clients.	Cost
Project participants seek growth hence there is need for constant training at different levels. Hence, **budgets** should include these **costs,** as the project is temporary and the participants.	Cost
We want to be empowered for taking decisions and allow us to take calculated risk for innovative activities, hence time and cost need **included in the budget**. The success will only help in **reduction** of the time **and cost,** not only for this instant but for all future similar projects.	Cost
The sustainable certainty in regard to future business is critical so that **investment** can be made in research and development that could **benefit** the main contractor as well as the end customer as well.	Cost
The contract **negotiations** with OEMs are basically **based on the cost** basis, thereby nullifying effects of any innovative approach as this requires uncertain cost and time. These are mainly scope related issues, which is also resolved on comprise basis rather than of Win – Win terms.	Cost
Several times **payments** become issues with the vendors/ OEM as they delay **the payments** due to various documentations requirements. These requirements were neither informed to us on placement of the order nor same it **mentioned in the contract,** yet payments are held up.	Cost

Sample Quotes	Factor
We need **to produce product**, what **is required by our customers** and not our engineers want to provide.	Customer satisfaction
Most of the issues get resolved in the **informal environment** as the participants are relaxed and ready to explore the possibilities for the solution to project related issues.	Environment – communication
We are unable to devote to project activities adequately **due to various service** non-functional **activities**; hence schedule gets affected and in our absence the decision is pending thus snow balling all the pressure from top to lower management.	Environment – internal
Lower management project participants were unable to take the **required necessary pressure** during peak time of the project and they preferred operational assignments.	Environment – internal
Due to the **weak organisation** matrix, ego management of the department head becomes a big **issue** for the project manager for smooth execution of projects.	Environment – internal
Sometimes, to meet the objectives set by their superiors, they **deviated** from **the processes** as those were in the interest of the **organisation**.	Environment – internal
Project success depends upon the stake holders, hence prior to start of the project, if **stake holder analysis** is undertaken then it will help in managing them appropriately **as per their needs**. By doing so there will be less issues during the project execution and acceptance of project on completion.	External and internal environment
Pokhran test was a critical success to country however this had given set back to the defence procurements.	External and internal environment

Sample Quotes	Factor
The project progress is affected by external factors such as central/ state policies, the political influence in the system, international environmental requirements, economic conditions, fluctuation in currency, etc. Therefore, there is a need for international cooperation to boost better trade for meeting the requirements set by the clients.	External and internal environment
The projects that are undertaken for the government sectors become difficult to perform due to interference of **several external agencies**. Sometime the files have to be approved by **ministry/ ministries** thus delay in the project which is unaccounted, and yard has to bear the penalty.	External and internal environment
Multiple agencies involvement in **government** projects is very infuriating; if there is testing of major equipment then it involves approximately **12-14 different agencies**. It is a mini project by itself to ensure that all are available else the testing cannot proceed.	External and internal environment
OEM should help them in improving managerial **capabilities of their management** and with appropriate technology for better **procedures and policies.**	External and internal environment
We are **hardly informed about the projects** for which the materials are being procured; hence we are unable to contribute anything towards **specific projects as an organisation.**	External and internal environment
Vendor/ OEM on bulk procurement should do **proper due diligence** as this will lessen post sale issues in regard to **project specific documentations**. Some time it becomes impossible to attend to such requirements.	External and internal environment
The **Pokhran test** has taken us back by five years in technology.	External environment

Sample Quotes	Factor
The vessel life cycle is mainly dependent upon the availability of imported spares, and most of the time availability of these get affected due to **sanctions and relationship with the respective country.**	External environment
The strategic shift of the **relationship between countries** delays our project drastically, such as our relationship with US, is leading to the projects delay in Russia.	External environment
Innovative approach in the project management can provide drastic changes to the project performance, hence calculated risk should be allowed for such activities.	Innovation
The intangibles related to **the team**, handling the project is key to the project success. **A motivated team** ensures that the lower management is proactive in the activities being performed, thus improving the project performance.	Internal environment
Coordination, with other departments involved were the major delays in regard to the completion of interrelated activities.	Internal environment
Project participants form **other departments** were more inclined towards their respective **departmental objectives** than the project objectives such as procurement - cost reduction, production - utilisation, quality assurance – non-deviation to process, etc.	Internal environment
Project team members need to have specific domain knowledge with the project requirement skills. In addition to that they need to have **high moral and ethical values.**	Moral and ethical values
A motivated team can do wonders to projects; the performance depends upon the percentage of **motivated team members**. It is very difficult to have 100% motivated team members.	Motivation

Sample Quotes	Factor
Being in government sector, **privileges** related to education to children, medical facilities, conveyance facilities etc. should also be provided or the salary should be at par with the private organisation.	Motivation
The organisation structure disables us the **empowerment** for the informal communication with stakeholders, thereby delaying the decision-making and affecting the project.	Motivation and internal environment
Most of our team members leave the **organisation** to private sector due to the **cultur**al related issues such as to decision-making, empowerment, rigid mindset, risk averse and compensation.	Motivation and internal environment
The major reasons of **attrition** in the project team at lower level are due to **the job role and compensation**. It is very difficult to make them understand that there needs to be **organic growth** to acquire the necessary skills set.	Motivation and internal environment
Encouragement to **lower-level workforce** needs to **be promoted** to the higher levels so that ground level requirements need is understood and appropriate decisions are taken for better project performance.	Organisation culture
The change in the ongoing **operational processes** is resisted by the functional level team due to waste of time and extra efforts to be undertaken for the activity.	Organisation culture
Most of the time our **tenure is for three years** and in the first 4-6 months. During this period, we are in **the process of taking** over and understand the dynamics of the project. Similarly during the end of tenure, around 4-6 months is for the handing over and winding up the office as well as the at personal front. Therefore only two years of the productive output can be provided.	Organisation culture /Internal environment

Sample Quotes	Factor
To improve the performance, the time and cost are being curtailed; this is affecting the project performance as **team building activities** are neglected. Therefore they intend to keep the same team for similar projects. Since the team participants have to grow, the same team cannot be kept for long time. This is hampering the project performance.	Organisation culture/ Structure
Few of the **qualified vendors** become nuisance to us from their **reselection** to project execution and even post completion.	Procurement
Project performance is dependent upon the **project manager skills** and his/ her team.	Project Manager
The **traits** preferred for project manager are more of **situational leadership** with high project management quotient.	Project Manager
Proper and timely decision from the **middle management** would improve the project performance, we observe that most of the time, decisions are changed abruptly in regard to the project requirements leading to inter and intra-organisation conflicts.	Project Manager
There is lack of the **appositeness** in regard to the authority, responsibility and accountability.	Project Manager
Project manager is key factor to **project success** as he/she is the focal point and decision-making authority for project on behalf of the key stake holder such as, customer, project sponsor, top management, key members of the project team.	Project Manager
We take formal acceptance from our customer as well as partners, prior to **appointing the project manager**, thereby ensuring buy-in in regard to the skill set requirement, and confidence for the project execution.	Project Manager

Sample Quotes	Factor
The project should meet the **required quality of the product** as per the set standards and there would be no compromise on the quality of the functionality of the product.	Quality
Scope is the critical **success criteria** as this defines the time, cost and the quality attribute of the project.	Scope
Most of the project failures are due to the **misinterpretation of the project scope**, since the contract is based on the macro scope and with verbal acceptance during contract formulation, however same are not accepted while execution of the project.	Scope
Many a times customer forgets to add **scope in the contract**, and post award expect us to provide the same without cost and schedule delay.	Scope
Since you are OEM we expect you to know the specifics of the contract even if not provided in the **contract scope**. Else this should have highlighted during the contract finalisation as you are the expert in the product.	Scope
If the project should also be undertaken for socio-economic **requirements**, disregarding the iron triangle, if it is **benefiting the humanity**, the best example is the Bada Imambara.	Success Criteria
Timely completion of the project with the latest technology and better life-cycle support of the ships/submarines from all the OEMs globally is necessary. Budget is not a constraint however **meeting higher project objective is important**, in terms of technology and product life cycle.	Success Criteria
Time required to build a warship is too high, and technologies adopted are superseded by better ones, thus defeating the **objective set** for building a vessel/platform.	Success Criteria

Sample Quotes	Factor
Without defining **the timeline**, the project will cease to exist.	Time
Schedule of every project is critical to the organisation success as, project cycle time will define order intakes.	Time
If **schedule is affected,** then the cost of the project is affected drastically hence it schedule impacts success a lot.	Time
Trust plays the key role in the cooperation of the team leading to better project performance.	Trust
Project performance is based on the teamwork, and **better team**work is only possible if there is **existence of the belief with each other**.	Trust
Even though the end customer wants the proven OEM, just for cost benefits, main contractors introduce new suppliers without realising the life-cycle related issues. We **feel let down** as for several years we have invested in the R& D of product development in association with the end customer.	Trust
Asking quotes only for the negotiation purpose and then further negotiating with their competitors diluted the **trust** factor.	Trust

Note

Literature Cited

The author wishes the readers of this book to focus more on the case studies, hence cited literature has not been provided in this book. The literature cited in this book is provided in the final book, restricting any duplication in both the book. The readers, when analysing the cases in the final book can refer the cited literature for in-depth understanding of the context by the respective authors.

Case Study Questionnaire

The questionnaire of the case as stated earlier in methodology is key to the success of any study/ research, hence same has also been provided in the final book. Author intends the readers to understand the dynamics of the cases initially, and then check the questionnaire how the case studies outcome was arrived from the questionnaire when analysing the cases in the final book can refer the cited literature for in-depth understanding of the context by the respective authors.

Publications

- VivekanandMBankolli(2011), *"BlueWaterNavalDocumentation –IETM,"* Proceedings of Seminar on Naval Documentation – Indian Navy (INHS Ashwini Mumbai), 18-19 Feb

- Vivekanand M Bankolli and Karuna Jain (2012), *"Impact of Intangibles in Marine Projects – A Case study,"* Proceedings of the PMSA conference, Johannesburg, South Africa, 17-19 Sep

- Vivekanand M Bankolli and Karuna Jain (2014), *"Interplay of Tangible and Intangible factors in project management: A case study of marine Project"* - Proceedings of Third International scientific Conference on project management in Baltic countries, University of Lativa, Riga.10-11Apr.

- Vivekanand M Bankolli and Karuna Jain (2017), *Tangible & Intangible success factors in Marine Construction Project*, NICMAR, Journal of construction management, Jun.

- Vivekanand M Bankolli and Karuna Jain (2019), *Intangible Success Factors Key to Marine Projects Performance – A Bipolar Case Study*, PMI India Research & Academic Conference, IIM Kozhikode, 28 Feb -02 Mar.

- Vivekanand M Bankolli and Karuna Jain (2022), *Success Factors Key to Marine Projects Performance – A Bipolar Case Study*, Journal of Engineering, Project, and Production management (EPPM-Journal) EPPM Conference, Athens, Greece, 12- 14 Oct.